CONTENTS

South & Cen[tral]
Lake District

WALKED AND WRITTEN BY JOHN WATSON.
SERIES CONCEPT AND DESIGN: MALCOLM PARKER.
ARTWORK AND DESIGN: RACHEL PAXTON & ANDREW FALLON.

PUBLISHED BY WALKS OF DISCOVERY LTD.,
1 MARKET PLACE, MIDDLETON-IN-TEESDALE,
CO. DURHAM, DL12 0QG. TEL: (01833) 640638.

PRINTED IN ENGLAND.
ISBN 0-86309-129-6.
COPYRIGHT © WALKS OF DISCOVERY LIMITED 1995.

C000121453

[DIFFICU]LTY:
[Easy), 4: Easy to Moderate
[M]oderate, 6: Moderate, 7: Moderate to Strenuous
8: Strenuous, 9: Strenuous, 10: Extremely Strenuous

IMPORTANT: Please note that these above gradings and the time lengths quoted below are based on the personal experience of the author and may vary significantly between individual walkers

How to use this Guide

This guide must only be used by the most serious of hill walkers who are fully prepared, equipped and experienced at walking in such demanding and difficult mountainous terrain.

■ **1** CHOOSE YOUR ROUTE Study the general location map opposite indicating our selection of 15 walk routes, then consult their individual route summary, background information, route description and route map before making your personal choice. Each 'circular' walk starts and finishes at the same point for your convenience.

■ **2** CHECK THE ROUTE SUITABILITY Carefully study your selected route to ensure that it is suitable for you, but particularly the weakest member of your party. To do this also consider the grading system for length and degree of difficulty for each route on the contents page - as well as the ascent, descent and cross-section information detailed on each individual walk description.

■ **3** CHECK THE WEATHER CONDITIONS Before you set out it is essential that you check the current and developing weather conditions. In addition, you should consider the Walking and Safety Tips on page 66. Also be aware of the telephone numbers of the emergency services.

■ **4** USE WITH AN ORDNANCE SURVEY MAP This guide is designed to be used with the relevant 1:25 000 scale O.S. Maps of the area. Grid references are used with the route descriptions in the guide.

■ **5** USING THE MAP AND ROUTE DESCRIPTION TOGETHER This guide is designed so that the route map and route description are on facing pages so that they may be viewed from one side of a map case, with the relevant 1:25 000 Ordnance Survey Map folded to the appropriate area viewed from the other side of the map case.

■ **6** USING THE ROUTE SECTIONS Each route is divided into a number of logical lettered sections which are clearly marked on the route map, in the route descriptions and on the cross-section. These should help you navigate your route.

■ **7** FOLLOWING THE ROUTE The detailed, concise route descriptions are clearly numbered in both the text and on the route map to help you locate your position.

■ **8** SHORT CUTS It is always best to plan for the unexpected and to be prepared for any eventuality. To assist you we have suggested some short cut alternatives should they be required.

Tourist Information

(NP) = National Park. **(S)** = Seasonal.
AMBLESIDE (S) The Old Courthouse, Church Street.
Tel: (015394) 32582
AMBLESIDE National Trust, Rothay Holme, Rothay Rd.
Tel: (015394) 35599
BARROW-IN-FURNESS Forum 28, Duke Street.
Tel: (01229) 870156
BOWNESS-ON-WINDERMERE (S) Glebe Road.
Tel: (015394) 42895
CONISTON (S) 16 Yewdale Road.
Tel: (015394) 41533
EGREMONT Lowes Court Gallery, 12 Main Street.
Tel: (01946) 820693
GLENRIDDING (NP) (S) Main Car Park.
Tel: (017684) 82414
GRANGE-OVER-SANDS (S) Victoria Hall, Main Street.
Tel: (015395) 34026
GRASMERE (NP) (S) Red Bank Road.
Tel: (015394) 35245
GRASMERE National Trust Information Centre,
Church Stile. Tel: (015394) 35621
HAWKSHEAD (S) Main Car Park.
Tel: (015394) 36525
KENDAL Town Hall, Highgate.
Tel: (01539) 725758
MILLOM (S) Millom Folk Museum.
Tel: (01229) 772555
SEATOLLER (NP) (S) Seatoller Barn, Borrowdale.
Tel: (017687) 77294
ULVERSTON Coronation Hall, County Square.

Tel: (01229) 587120
WATERHEAD (S) The Car Park, Waterhead.
Tel: (015394) 32729
WINDERMERE Victoria Street.
Tel: (015394) 46499
WHITEHAVEN Market Hall, Market Place.
Tel: (01946) 695678

Useful Information

FELL RESCUE SERVICES
Contact the Police. Tel: 999
WEATHER FORECAST
National Park recorded information
(including details of fell-top conditions)
Tel: (017687) 75757
RADIO CUMBRIA
Frequencies: medium 397 (North), 358 (Central &
South), 206 (West), VHF 104.2 (Central)
and 95 - 96 (all other areas).
LONG DISTANCE WALKERS ASSOCIATION
117 Higher Lane, Rainford, St Helens, Merseyside, WA11 8BQ.
Tel: (01744) 882638
DISCOVERY VISITOR CENTRE
1 Market Place,
Middleton-in-Teesdale,
County Durham, DL12 0QG.
Tel & Fax: (01833) 640638
For details of current and forthcoming
Walks of Discovery walking guides.

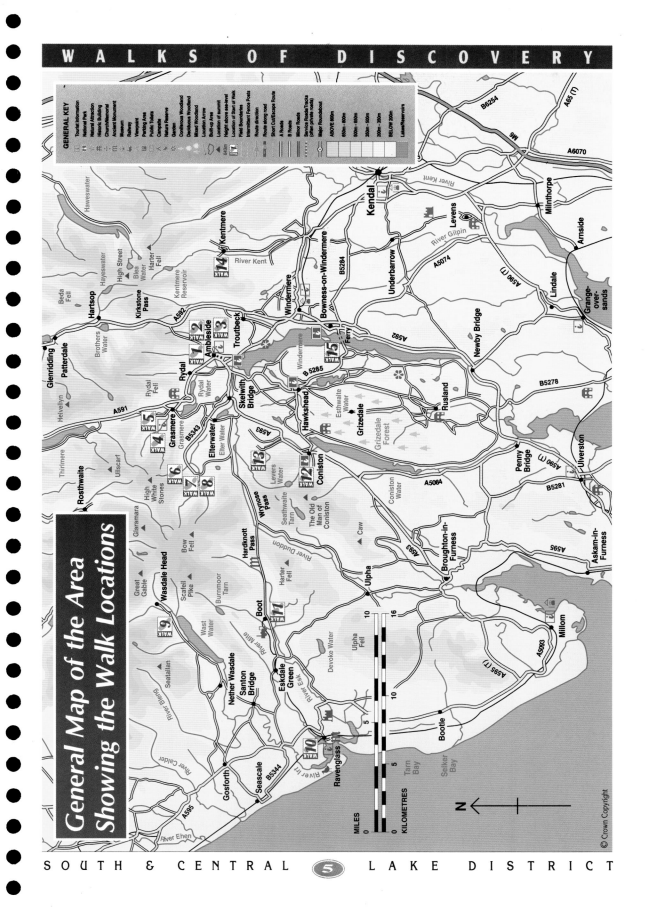

General Map of the Area
Showing the Walk Locations

GENERAL KEY

Tourist Information
National Park
Natural Attraction
Historic Building
Church/Memorial
Ancient Monument
Museum
Railway
Vineyard
Parking Area
Public Toilets
Campsite
Garden
Nature Reserve
Mixed Woodland
Coniferous Woodland
Deciduous Woodland
Location Arrow
Location of summit
Built-up Area
Height above sea-level
Field Boundaries
Intermittant Fence Posts
Route direction
Route along road
Short Cut/Escape Route
Service Route/Tracks (often private roads)
A Roads
B Roads
Minor Roads
Major Roundabout

ABOVE 600m
650m - 600m
500m - 650m
350m - 500m
350m - 350m
BELOW 200m
Lakes/Reservoir

© Crown Copyright

HIGH SWEDEN BRIDGE-
HIGH PIKE-
DOVE CRAG-
FAIRFIELD-
NAB SCAR
11.7 miles (18.8km)

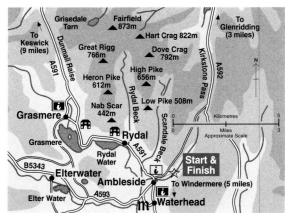

Route Details

Distance	11.7 miles (18.8km)
Degree of Difficulty	Strenuous
Ascent	1,030m (3,377ft)
Time	8 hours

Start and Finish Points

Rydal Road car park (GR 376047) Ambleside.
From Keswick take the A591 (S) along the eastern shore of Thirlmere and through the village of Rydal. On entering Ambleside pass Charlotte Mason College on the left. The car park entrance is on the right across Stock Ghyll opposite the entrance to the college.

From Windermere take the A591 (N) and go through Ambleside. The car park is on the left on leaving the town.

Maps Needed

OS Outdoor Leisure No 7 (1:25 000)
OS Outdoor Leisure No 5 (1:25 000)
OS Landranger No 90 (1:50 000)

Parking Facilities

Rydal Road pay and display car park is at the northern end of Ambleside, its entrance bridging Stock Ghyll. Toilets. Refreshments and Tourist Information Centre in the town.

Short Cuts

At (5) turn left (S), descending the fell to cross Low Sweden Bridge over Scandale Beck. From Nook End Farm continue (S) down a minor road to turn right on the Kirkstone Road, briefly, to the A591, and return to the car park.

Route Summary

This popular traverse of a high-level horseshoe ridge, circling the Rydal valley, passes over eight summits en route. It is a magnificent aerial promenade, affording panoramic views of distant mountains and lakes, as well as a close-up study of volcanic mountain structures which range from the desolate to the pastoral. Starting from the old part of Ambleside, there is a steady climb up a scenic lane along Scandale Beck as far as the delightful hump-backed High Sweden Bridge. An ascent onto the narrow ridge and over Low Pike and High Pike leads to the summits of Dove Crag, Hart Crag and Fairfield. From the northern and eastern escarpment rims of these three peaks emanate rocky ridges and wild corries ringed with rugged, scarred cliffs.

A quiet moment in the normally bustling town of Ambleside

The descent from Fairfield follows a grassy carpet down a ridge over Great Rigg and Heron Pike with superb views over the vale of Grasmere. At its end is Nab Scar overlooking the charms of Rydal Water. A steep serpentine path drops down to Rydal Mount, one-time home to William Wordsworth. A quiet amble along a sylvan valley through Rydal Park completes a memorable walk.

Interesting Features

LANDFORMS Fairfield is situated on a horseshoe of ridges and peaks enclosing the Rydal valley. The eastern spur of the horseshoe, rising from Ambleside, is a narrow rocky ridge, leading (N) and bounded by the Rydal valley (W) and Scandale (E). It passes over the two level tops of Low Pike and High Pike to the equally flat top of Dove Crag. In contrast to the grassy slopes of the southern ridge, Dove Crag has an eastern facade of rugged dark cliffs which descend into the lovely valley of Dovedale, and then down to Brothers Water in Patterdale. Continuing on the ridge (NW), after a depression, is the rocky summit of Hart Crag which overlooks three valleys: (SW) its bouldered slopes drop into Rydal valley; (N) a sheer wall of crags plunges into the desolate hanging valley of Ling Cove; and (NE) is a long descending ridge which provides the divide between the barren Deepdale and pastoral Dovedale.

The centrepiece of the curving ridge is Fairfield, whose northern face is characteristic of the Borrowdale Volcanic structure. A tangle of scree, precipices and combes are intersected by a thin steep-sided ridge, containing the summit of Cofa Pike and leading (N) to St Sunday Crag. (NW) its steep rocky slope drops down to Grisedale Tarn at the head of Grisedale, a valley which pursues a course (NE) into Patterdale and the head of Ullswater. In complete contrast, the ridge which forms the western spur of the horseshoe and intersects Rydal (E) and the Rothay valley (W), is fringed with grassy slopes, as it descends over Great Rigg and Heron Pike to Nab Scar, the last prominence on the ridge. The craggy south face of Nab Scar falls abruptly down to Rydal Water in the Rothay valley.

HISTORY The village of Rydal owes its fame to the Wordsworth connection. After Grasmere, the poet lived at Rydal Mount from 1813 until his death in 1850 at the age of eighty. His family remained at Rydal Mount, now owned by his great-great-granddaughter. Once a C16th farm cottage, it was extended in the mid C18th. The house takes its name from a mound in front of it which was the site of a beacon. The house, and the grounds designed by Wordsworth, are open to the public.

Dora's Field behind St Mary's Church was given by the poet to his favourite daughter. Tended by the National Trust, the field is covered by a carpet of daffodils in the spring.

For Ambleside, consult Walk 2 on page 11 (History).

Bridge House, a C17th summerhouse, spanning Stock Ghyll

VIEWPOINTS On this high-level horseshoe ridge with its eight summits, the panoramic views are magnificent throughout. To select individual viewpoints would be exhausting, so Fairfield, as the highest point, must serve as a general direction-finder for other prominences. (N) is St Sunday Crag and (NE) beyond Ullswater, are Beda Fell and Angletarn Pikes, whilst the High Street range occupies the skyline (E). Froswick, Ill Bell and Yoke follow a long line as far as Red Screes (SE). Looking (S), a section of Windermere can be seen with Wansfell Pike up to the left. (SW) the summit of The Old Man of Coniston and Wetherlam are prominent. Moving round (W), the skyline contains the serrated edge of Crinkle Crags and the pyramid of Bow Fell, fronted by the Langdale Pikes and backed by the Scafell range. (W) is Great Gable with Pillar and the High Stile range to the right, followed by Dale Head, Hindscarth, Robinson, Grasmoor, Crag Hill and Grisedale Pike. (NW) beginning with Dollywagon Pike, stretches the long ridge over Helvellyn, beyond which is a glimpse of Blencathra.

For splendid aerial views over Rydal Water, the best vantage-points are (W) from Sweden Bridge Lane and (S) from the perimeter of Nab Scar.

Cross-Section of the Route

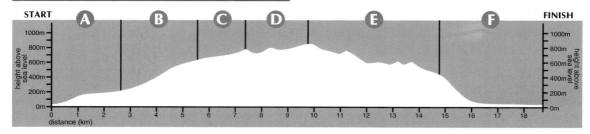

START   A   B   C   D   E   F   FINISH

height above sea level — 1000m, 800m, 600m, 400m, 200m, 0m

distance (km) — 0 1 2 3 4 5 6 7 8 9 10 11 12 13 14 15 16 17 18

Route Description

SECTION A	1.7 miles (2.7km)		
Destination	High Sweden Bridge (GR 379067)		
Ascent	230m(754ft)	Descent	0m(0ft)

■ **1** Start by leaving the car park entrance. Go right on the A591 for 30m. Turn left to cross the road. Go up the Kirkstone Road opposite. Pass the first junction on the left. Continue uphill on the road.

■ **2** Turn left, 75m after a left bend in the road at a sign to High Sweden Bridge. Proceed (N) up a 'no-through' minor road for 400m.

■ **3** Pass through a field-gate. Go uphill on the walled stony track of Sweden Bridge Lane for 900m. Pass through a field-gate into woodland. Continue ahead on the level track for 600m. Pass through a field-gate onto open fell. Continue for 150m. Fork left, off the track, down to High Sweden Bridge.

SECTION B	2 miles (3.2km)		
Destination	High Pike (GR 374088)		
Ascent	376m(1233ft)	Descent	0m(0ft)

■ **4** Turn left across the bridge over Scandale Beck. Immediately turn right over a stile adjacent to a wicket-gate. Immediately turn left (WSW) uphill, along a broken wall on the right. Pass over a high ladder-stile after 200m. Go straight ahead for 125m.

■ **5** Turn right (N) on a gradually ascending path over open fell which bends left, passing through a broken wall as it meanders up over Low Brock Crags.

■ **6** Turn right (NNW) at a pathway junction on High Brock Crags. Follow the wall on the left. At a depression, pass through a low stone wall. Go through a wall gap as the path ascends. Keep left at a large cairn on the left. Go up onto a small grassy plateau. Bear right away from the wall, the path bending left onto the summit of Low Pike (508m/1,666ft).

■ **7** From the summit, go ahead, along the wall on the left. Go over a ladder-stile at a depression 200m ahead. Climb a rocky path, keeping the wall on the left onto the summit of High Pike (656m/2,152ft).

SECTION C	1.2 miles (2km)		
Destination	Dove Crag (GR 375105)		
Ascent	136m(446ft)	Descent	0m(0ft)

■ **8** From the summit, go up the ridge on a path along the wall on the left. Pass over a stile in a fence coming in from the right. Continue ahead for 400m. The summit cairn of Dove Crag (792m/2,598ft) is on the right on a broad plateau. For views down the crags into Patterdale continue ahead (N) away from the wall for 250m. Return to (9).

SECTION D	1.6 miles (2.6km)		
Destination	Fairfield (GR 359117)		
Ascent	208m(682ft)	Descent	137m(449ft)

■ **9** Bend left (NW) on the ridge with the wall on the left. Descend into a depression. Ascend steeply up crags, where the wall on the left ends. Climb to the summit of Hart Crag (822m/2,696ft).

■ **10** Descend (NW) the boulder-strewn side of Hart Crag. Cross over a grassy depression. The path bends left, gradually ascending a slope onto a broad plateau summit. Bend right to the summit cairn and shelter of Fairfield (873m/2,863ft).

SECTION E	2.9 miles (4.6km)		
Destination	Nab Scar (GR 355072)		
Ascent	80m(262ft)	Descent	483m(1584ft)

■ **11** Turn left (S) at the shelter, amidst a confusing number of cairns. Go off the summit plateau on a clearly descending ridge path (SSW). Cross a depression to ascend to the summit cairn of Great Rigg (766m/2,512ft).

■ **12** Continue ahead, descending the ridge (SSW). Gradually bend left (SSE) where the path levels out. Ascend gradually (SSW) to the top of Heron Pike (612m/2,007ft).

■ **13** Proceed ahead (SSW) downhill. Pass Lord Crag on the right. The cairned path bends left along a broken wall on the right. Just before a wall and ladder-stile, a small diversion up right is required to gain the summit of Nab Scar (442m/1,450ft). Return to the main path.

SECTION F	2.3 miles (3.7km)		
Destination	Ambleside (GR 376047)		
Ascent	0m(0ft)	Descent	410m(1345ft)

■ **14** Continue ahead on the path to pass over the ladder-stile ahead. The clear path ahead zig-zags (SE) steeply down the south face of Nab Scar. Bend left near the bottom to pass over a ladder-stile with a small conifer plantation on the left.

■ **15** Go down a twisting path between walls. Pass through a kissing-gate adjacent to a field-gate. Bend right (SSE) with a cottage on the right to go through a field-gate. Filter right onto a minor road. Continue downhill, passing the large white house of Rydal Mount on the right.

■ **16** Turn left (ENE), 80m after Rydal Mount, at a footpath sign and a wall sign to Rydal Hall Campsite and Youth Centre. Proceed along a broad track with Rydal Hall over on the right. The track bends right between buildings. Bear left to cross a stone bridge over Rydal Beck.

■ **17** The track bends right between buildings at a wall sign to Ambleside. It bends left with a campsite on the right. Proceed (SE) through Rydal Park. Go over a stile adjacent to a field-gate 400m after the campsite. Continue ahead (SSE) on the track, eventually running (S) alongside Scandale Beck on the left. At the end of the track pass through ornamental wrought-iron gates with a lodge-house on the the right.

■ **18** Cross over the busy A591 Keswick to Windermere road. Turn left (SSE) on a pathway alongside the road. Cross Scandale Bridge. After 700m arrive at the car park on the right.

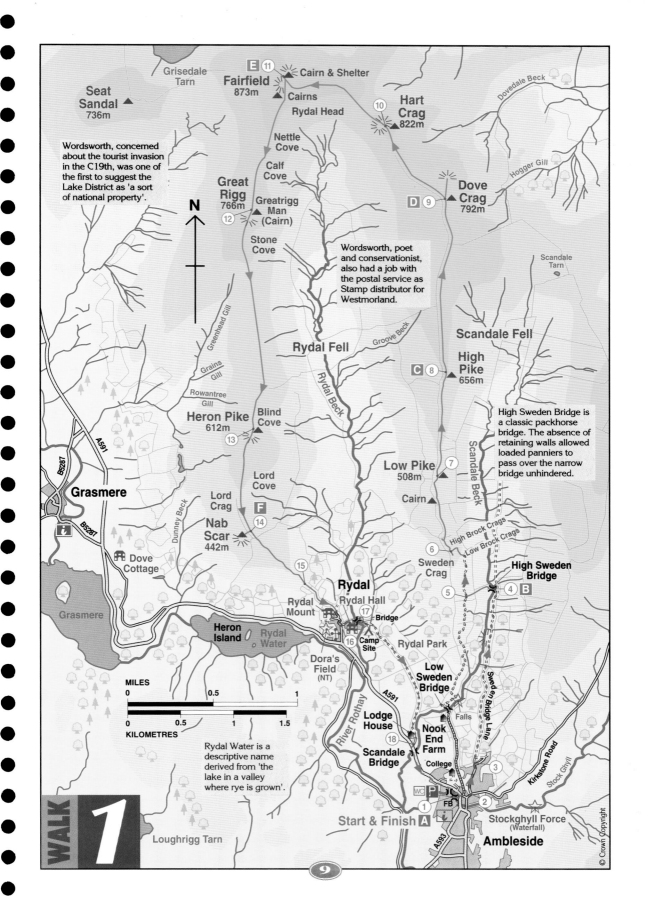

Seat Sandal ▲ 736m

Grisedale Tarn

E 11 ☀ Cairn & Shelter
Fairfield 873m
▲ Cairns
Rydal Head

Dovedale Beck

10 ☀ Hart Crag ▲ 822m

Hogger Gill

Wordsworth, concerned about the tourist invasion in the C19th, was one of the first to suggest the Lake District as 'a sort of national property'.

Nettle Cove

Calf Cove

Great Rigg 766m
12 ▲ Greatrigg Man (Cairn)

Stone Cove

☀ Dove Crag ▲ 792m
D 9

Scandale Tarn

N ↑

Wordsworth, poet and conservationist, also had a job with the postal service as Stamp distributor for Westmorland.

Rydal Fell

Groove Beck

Scandale Fell

High Pike 656m
C 8 ▲

Greenhead Gill

Grains Gill

Rowantree Gill

Rydal Beck

Heron Pike 612m
13 ☀
Blind Cove

High Sweden Bridge is a classic packhorse bridge. The absence of retaining walls allowed loaded panniers to pass over the narrow bridge unhindered.

Lord Cove

Low Pike 508m
7

Grasmere

B5287

Cairn ▲

Lord Crag
F 14
Nab Scar 442m ☀

Dunney Beck

6
High Brock Crags
Low Brock Crags

Sweden Crag

5

High Sweden Bridge
4 B

Scandale Beck

Dove Cottage

15

Rydal
Rydal Hall
17 Bridge

Rydal Mount

Heron Island
Grasmere
Rydal Water

16 △ Camp Site

Rydal Park

Sweden Bridge Lane

Dora's Field (NT)

Low Sweden Bridge

River Rothay

A591

Lodge House

18

Scandale Bridge

Nook End Farm

College

Falls

Kirkstone Road

Stock Ghyll

3

MILES
0   0.5   1

KILOMETRES
0   0.5   1   1.5

Rydal Water is a descriptive name derived from 'the lake in a valley where rye is grown'.

WC P
1 A
FB

2

Start & Finish A

Stockghyll Force (Waterfall)

A593

Ambleside

Loughrigg Tarn

© Crown Copyright

WALK 1

9

2

AMBLESIDE-STOCKGHYLL FORCE-WANSFELL PIKE-TROUTBECK-JENKIN CRAG

7 miles (11.2km)

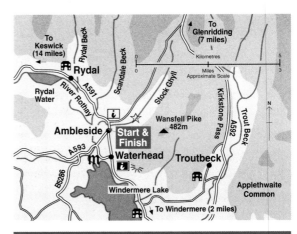

Route Details

Distance	7 miles (11.2km)
Degree of Difficulty	Easy
Ascent	556m (1,824ft)
Time	5 hours

Start and Finish Points

Rydal Road car park (GR 376047), Ambleside.

From Keswick take the A591 (S) and the car park is 200 metres on the right, opposite Charlotte Mason College on entering Ambleside.

From Windermere take the A591 (N) and on going through Ambleside the car park is on the left on leaving the town.

Maps Needed

OS Outdoor Leisure No 7 (1:25 000)
OS Landranger No 90 (1:50 000)

Parking Facilities

Rydal Road pay and display car park is at the north end of Ambleside. Toilets. Refreshments and Tourist Information Centre in the town.

Short Cuts

There are no major short cuts on this walk, but to visit Stockghyll Force only, then:

At (7) continue downhill with Stock Ghyll on the right as far as (4). Then follow the outward route back to the car park.

This is a popular short circular walk of 1.2 miles from the car park in Ambleside, with opportunities to explore and picnic in picturesque surroundings.

Route Summary

This absorbing walk begins up a wooded ravine to the top of Stock Ghyll Force, one of Ambleside's major attractions. From here there is quite a steep climb up to the summit of Wansfell Pike. The effort is rewarded with a superb view down Windermere, England's longest lake. This high-level route continues on a sinuous course down the fellside onto the walled Nanny Lane, and into one of Lakeland's most attractive villages, Troutbeck. It is renowned for its C17th and C18th statesmen farmhouses, one of which, Town End is owned by the National Trust, open to the public and well worth a visit. The lower-level return route, on the terraced bridleway path of Robin Lane high above Windermere, passes through the delightful Skelghyll Wood, touching on Jenkin Crag, another magnificent vantage-point for views over the lake.

A glimpse of Stockghyll Force from its woodland ravine

Cascading falls, shaded woodland, open fell, a rocky summit of modest height, ancient lanes, a town and village with long histories, an ancient farmhouse, and above all breathtaking aerial views of Windermere, all combine to make this an unforgettable walk.

Interesting Features

LANDFORMS High to the north of Ambleside is Caudale Moor from which emanates three southerly ridges. The most westerly and longest of these is crossed by the Kirkstone Pass road over a wide depression. The ridge descends south, and is then interrupted by rising and narrowing over two elevated spurs, Wansfell and Wansfell Pike, before descending gradually to Jenkin Crag, where it drops more abruptly to the eastern shore of Windermere. Wansfell Pike is situated on the south-western edge of the ridge. From its rocky summit the slopes are extensive, especially to the east where streams flow over marshy ground down into the Troutbeck valley. South-west, a rather more abrupt descent leads down to the steep-sided ravine of Stockghyll Force before encountering Ambleside.

HISTORY The market town of Ambleside, at the centre of the Lake District, had two Roman forts at Galava near the confluence of the rivers Brathay and Rothay. They served as midway staging-posts on the highest Roman road in Britain which linked Brougham (Brocavum) near Penrith to the east with the port of Ravenglass (Glannoventa) to the west.

Ambleside owes its early growth to Stock Ghyll which powered several mills. The former corn-mill, now a pottery and shop, dates from the C14th and corn was ground here into the C20th. Other ancient mills were a bobbin mill, bark-crushing mill, and a paper mill. A woollen-mill and fulling-mill enhanced the town's reputation for its wool sales.

Ambleside was granted a market charter in 1650, and though it contains some C17th buildings, its main expansion came about in the C19th during the Victorian tourist era when wealthy businessmen built their Italianate and Gothic villas close to the shores of Windermere. Lack of C19th controls lead to a sprawling form of development.

The dollshouse-like dwelling, Bridge House, spans Stock Ghyll in Ambleside. It was built in the C17th by the Braithwaites of Ambleside Hall to serve as a summerhouse and a means of crossing the ghyll. It is reputed that in the C19th a chair-repairer and his wife brought up six children in this tiny dwelling which now serves as a National Trust Information Centre.

The straggling village of Troutbeck, situated on a shelf above the Troutbeck valley, is a series of linked hamlets containing over a dozen C17th and early C18th statesman farmhouses. Its dwellings are clustered round a number of wells from which communal water-supplies were once obtained. At Town Head is the Queen's Head Inn with a mayoral parlour, scene of Troutbeck's mayor-making ceremony for over 200 years.

The National Trust property of Town End in Troutbeck belonged to the Browne family from when it was built in 1623. It is a fascinating and excellent example of a Lakeland yeoman farmer's house with its cylindrical chimneys, slate roof, oak-mullioned windows, lime-rendered stonework, wool barn and spinning gallery.

For Windermere, consult Walk 15 on page 63 (History).

Historic Troutbeck couched on a sheltered hillside shelf

VIEWPOINTS The modest summit of Wansfell Pike, and later Jenkin Crag, are excellent vantage-points for magnificent views over the length of Windermere. (SW) are the Old Man of Coniston and Wetherlam. (W) are the summits of Pike of Blisco, Crinkle Crags, the Scafells and Bow Fell. (WSW) can be seen Harrison Stickle, one of the Langdale Pikes, situated between the more distant tops of Great End and Great Gable. (NW) the Fairfield/Nab Scar ridge is prominent, whilst (N) there is a fine aspect of Red Screes. (NE) is Caudale Moor crowned by the summit of Thornthwaite Crag, to the right of which are the Kentmere fells.

Cross-Section of the Route

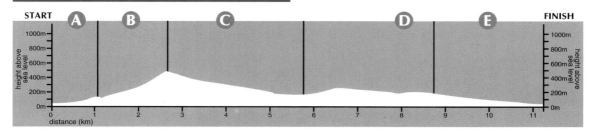

Route Description

SECTION A	0.7 miles (1.2km)		
Destination	Stockghyll Force (GR 384046)		
Ascent	100m(328ft)	Descent	0m(0ft)

■ **1** Start from the car park to the right of the toilets. Go over a footbridge onto the A591. Cross the road. Turn right (S). Go through Ambleside as far as the Salutation Hotel up on the left where the road bends sharply right.

■ **2** Go ahead on a narrow street (SE) between Barclays Bank and the Market Hall for 25m. Turn left at signs to the waterfalls, Stock Ghyll and Wansfell Pike. Follow up a minor road for 350m.

■ **3** Fork left, off the road, through an unmarked wall gap adjacent to a field-gate. Follow a woodland path (ENE) along Stock Ghyll on the left for 150m.

■ **4** Fork left down stone steps. Turn left across a footbridge over the gill. Immediately bear half-right up the wooded bankside. The path follows an iron fence on the right above the gill.

■ **5** Fork right at the top of the rise. Go down a narrow path along the fence to the foot of Stockghyll Force. Return to (5). Turn sharp right up the stepped bankside to the head of the falls.

SECTION B	1 mile (1.6km)		
Destination	Wansfell Pike (GR 394042)		
Ascent	334m(1096ft)	Descent	0m(0ft)

■ **6** Turn right across a stepped footbridge over the falls. Immediately turn right (WSW) along the iron fence on the right, descending over rocks for 100m.

■ **7** Take the left fork at a picnic-table. Go through a metal turnstile gate. Ahead, emerge from woodland onto a tarmac lane.

■ **8** Turn left (ENE) at a footpath sign to Kirkstone. Pass through a field-gate adjacent to a cattle-grid. Continue ahead for 170m.

■ **9** Turn right off the lane at a bench-seat on the left. Go over an iron ladder-stile at a sign to Troutbeck via Wansfell. Immediately cross a wooden stile. Continue ahead (E) uphill over grassland, bending right (SE) along the gill on the left. Pass over a high ladder-stile ahead.

■ **10** Go ahead over cross-paths. Ascend Wansfell parallel to the gill on the left.

■ **11** Go through a broken wall above the tree-line. Veer left at a large cairn on the left. Ford the shallow beck. Bear right, uphill, leaving the beck on the left. Ascend over rocky outcrops. Pass through a broken wall at a cairn on the left. Continue ahead uphill. Turn left at a cairn to the OS triangulation pillar on the summit of Wansfell Pike (484m/1,588ft).

SECTION C	1.6 miles (2.6km)		
Destination	Troutbeck Post Office (GR 407026)		
Ascent	0m(0ft)	Descent	414m(1358ft)

■ **12** Continue ahead for 25m. Turn right over a ladder-stile at a sign to Troutbeck via Nanny Lane.

Go ahead, leaving the wall on the left to follow the cairned path diagonally left (E) down the fell. Pass over a footbridge. Go through a metal kissing-gate when the path levels out. Go through another metal kissing-gate. Emerge onto Nanny Lane.

■ **13** Turn right (SE) down the walled track. Pass over a stile. Go through a wicket-gate. After another 20 metres, emerge onto the road.

■ **14** Turn right (SSW) along the road for 800m, passing through the village of Troutbeck as far as the Post Office on the right.

SECTION D	2 miles (3km)		
Destination	Jenkin Crag (GR 384029)		
Ascent	122m(400ft)	Descent	20m(66ft)

■ **15** Bear right, off the road, at a bridleway sign to Ambleside. Go up Robin Lane, climbing gradually and bending right (WNW) round the hillside. Ignore any branch paths for 0.8 miles.

■ **16** Bear left at a fork through a kissing-gate adjacent to two field-gates at a low level sign Skelgyhll/Ambleside via Jenkin Crag. Follow down a path (NW) along a wall on the left. Pass through a kissing-gate. Continue with the wall on the left for 200m.

■ **17** Ford a stream. Immediately turn sharp left up a rough path. Pass through a wall gap. Go downhill, bending round a ruined barn on the left. Pass through a wicket-gate at the bottom of the slope.

■ **18** Bear right to cross a bridge over Hol Beck. Immediately pass through a kissing-gate adjacent to a cattle-grid. Follow ahead on a driveway uphill along a wire fence for 200m.

■ **19** Pass round High Skelgyhll Farm on the right. Go through a metal field-gate at the up left corner. Pass through a walled enclosure to go through a field-gate. Follow a terraced path (W).

■ **20** Go through a field-gate 200m after the farm. Continue ahead uphill through Skelghyll Wood. Turn left at (21), through a wall gap, at a sign on the left indicating Jenkin Crag. Go ahead for 70m to the lip of the crag (168m/551ft).

SECTION E	1.7 miles (2.8km)		
Destination	Ambleside (GR 376047)		
Ascent	0m(0ft)	Descent	122m(400ft)

■ **21** Return to the main path. Turn left, along the wall on the left. Bear left, and round an S-bend. Take the higher right fork at the foot of the bend.

■ **22** Go down, later, across a bridge over Stencher Beck. Follow downhill along the beck, bending right away from it at the bottom of a slope.

■ **23** Emerge from woodland through a wall gap. Continue ahead (N) along woodland on the right. The path becomes a narrow tarmac road, bending left (WNW) between two houses. Bend right (NNW) downhill to emerge at crossroads.

■ **24** Filter right (N) along Old Lake Road.

■ **25** Filter right onto Lake Road (A591). Continue ahead to (2). Bend left to retrace the outward route to the car park.

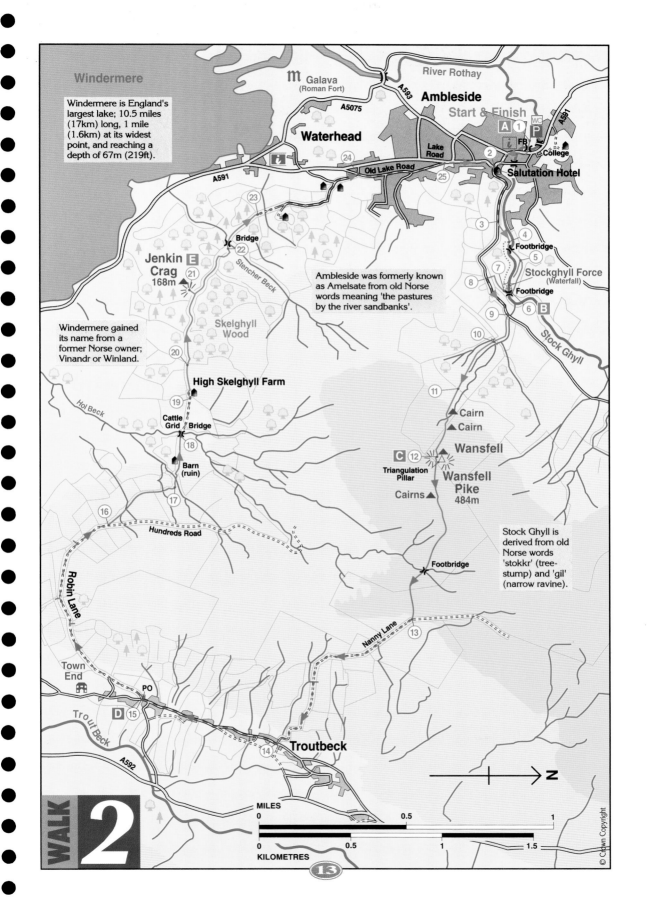

Windermere

Windermere is England's largest lake; 10.5 miles (17km) long, 1 mile (1.6km) at its widest point, and reaching a depth of 67m (219ft).

ⲙ Galava
(Roman Fort)

River Rothay

A593

Ambleside

Start & Finish

A ①

WC
P

i FB
College

A591

A5075

Waterhead

Lake Road

②

Salutation Hotel

Old Lake Road

A591

②④

②⑤

③

④

Footbridge

⑤

Stockghyll Force
(Waterfall)

②③

Bridge

②②

Jenkin Crag **E**
168m ②①

Stencher Beck

Ambleside was formerly known as Amelsate from old Norse words meaning 'the pastures by the river sandbanks'.

⑦

⑧

Footbridge

⑨

B

⑥

Stock Ghyll

Skelghyll Wood

Windermere gained its name from a former Norse owner; Vinandr or Winland.

②⓪

⑩

Hol Beck

High Skelghyll Farm

⑪

▲ Cairn
▲ Cairn

⑲

Cattle Grid

Bridge

⑱

Barn (ruin)

C ⑫

Triangulation Pillar

Wansfell

Wansfell Pike
484m

Cairns ▲

⑰

⑯

Hundreds Road

Footbridge

Stock Ghyll is derived from old Norse words 'stokkr' (tree-stump) and 'gil' (narrow ravine).

Robin Lane

Nanny Lane

⑬

Town End

PO

Trout Beck

D ⑮

⑭

Troutbeck

A592

→ z

W A L K

2

MILES
0   0.5   1

0   0.5   1   1.5
KILOMETRES

WALK 3

AMBLESIDE-
RYDAL CAVE-
LOUGHRIGG TARN-
LOUGHRIGG FELL-
MILLER BROW

7.2 miles (11.5km)

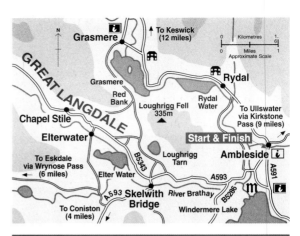

Route Details

Distance	7.2 miles (11.5km)
Degree of Difficulty	Easy
Ascent	254m (833ft)
Time	4.5 hours

Start and Finish Points

Rydal Road car park in Ambleside (GR 376047)

From Keswick take the A591 (S). On entering Ambleside, the car park is on the right opposite the entrance to Charlotte Mason College.

From Windermere take the A591 (N), go through Ambleside, and the car park is on the left.

Maps Needed

OS Outdoor Leisure No 7 (1:25 000)
OS Landranger No 90 (1:50 000)

Parking Facilities

Rydal Road pay and display car park is at the north end of Ambleside. Toilets. Refreshments and Tourist Information Centre in the town.

Short Cuts

At (13) at the end of Loughrigg Terrace turn left (SE) up a stony path. Keep ahead to the summit of Loughrigg Fell (335 metres/1,098ft). Continue (SE) on a path which meanders over the fell, crossing intersecting paths and passing to the left of a tiny tarn. Drop down the fellside to (21). Turn left to ford a rivulet. This route omits Loughrigg Tarn.

At (21) go straight ahead (NE) at the fork on a stony bridleway path. Proceed downhill to join the route at (26).

Route Summary

This is an easy walk on good paths along the lower slopes of Loughrigg Fell, involving gentle ascents onto fellside terraces from which there are outstandingly beautiful aerial views over Rydal Water, Grasmere, Loughrigg Tarn and Windermere. As Wordsworth lived most of his life in Grasmere and Rydal, it is to be assumed that this walk covers some of the paths that were followed by him. Undoubtedly much of the magnificent scenery served as a source of inspiration for his poetry. Indeed the superb view from Loughrigg Terrace over Grasmere and the Rothay Valley up to the distinctive pinnacle of Helm Crag and the surrounding fells was described by Wordsworth as 'a visionary scene'.

Secluded Loughrigg Tarn nestling below Loughrigg Fell

The walk has many contrasting ingredients: a feast of glorious views from wooded terraced paths; a delightful lane meandering along the course of the River Rothay; and a stretch of open fell. A particular highlight must be the vast man-made Rydal Cave encountered en route which provides a brush with a thriving industrial past, as well as an opportunity to explore its cathedral-like confines which contain a tarn inhabited by a small fish population.

Interesting Features

LANDFORMS Loughrigg Fell is a sprawling wedge of land of only moderate altitude with several modest summits. It stands almost isolated, occupying a position between Grasmere and Rydal Water in the Rothay valley (N) and the Brathay valley (S) at the entrance to Little Langdale. A narrow col links it with a long broad ridge proceeding north-west over Silver How, Sergeant Man, and terminating at High Raise.

Despite its low elevation, Loughrigg Fell is characteristic of the Borrowdale Volcanic series in that it is dotted with short rocky tors and tiny tarns.

HISTORY The River Rothay rises near Dunmail Raise, south of Thirlmere, passing through Grasmere and Rydal Water on its winding course south to Windermere. It is said that when Windermere's char and trout swim upstream to spawn, on reaching the confluence of the Rivers Rothay and Brathay at Ambleside, the char go up the Brathay and the trout up the Rothay. Whether this is true or not, the River Rothay has derived its name from the Norse meaning 'the river of the red one' or 'the trout river'.

The steep-sided valley of Glen Rothay contains the reeded Rydal Water which was gouged out by glacial ice, the residual debris forming the scenically enhancing islands dotted amidst its shallow waters, which do not exceed 17 metres (56ft) in depth. It was originally known as Routermere or Rothaymere after the River Rothay which flows through it.

On one of the northern lower shelves of Loughrigg Fell are the Rydal Caves, formerly quarried for their famous blue slate from which much of Ambleside is constructed. One of them contains a small tarn in its cavernous interior, 12 metres (40ft) in height, and so vast that it has frequently served as a venue for carol concerts.

The area is regarded as Wordsworth country because he lived at Dove Cottage, Grasmere and at Rydal Mount from 1799 to his death at the age of 80 in 1850. As a poet, Wordsworth was a symbol of the European Romantic Movement of the late C18th and early C19th. He was also a landscape designer, gardener, Distributor of Stamps for Westmorland, and writer of a guide to the Lake District published in 1810. In 1799, accompanied by fellow poet Samuel Taylor Coleridge, he went on a 'Pikteresk Toor' of Lakeland. As a conservationist, he was the first to advocate that the Lake District become 'a sort of national property', and though he complained about the number of visitors he probably did more than anyone to popularize Lakeland.

Grasmere lake is 1 mile long and 23 metres (75ft) at its deepest point. Wordsworth fished its waters for trout, pike and perch. In 1807 he described the scene over Grasmere from its shores, concluding that:

'....if unholy deeds
Ravage the world, tranquility is here!'

For Ambleside, consult Walk 2 on page 11 (History).

Silver How above Grasmere viewed from Loughrigg Terrace

VIEWPOINTS The traverse of the northern slopes of Loughrigg Fell affords spectacular views over Rydal Water and Grasmere backed by the long ridge leading west from Nab Scar above Rydal to the summit of Fairfield.

From Loughrigg Tarn on the southern slopes of the fell is the magnificent silhouette of the Langdale Pikes (NW).

The south-eastern heights of Loughrigg Fell is a superb vantage-point for aerial views over Ambleside and Lake Windermere.

Cross-Section of the Route

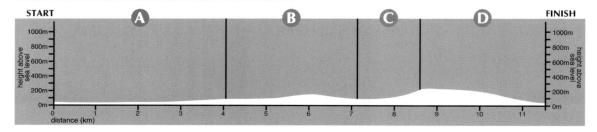

Route Description

SECTION A	2.4 miles (3.8km)		
Destination	Rydal Cave (GR 355057)		
Ascent	85m(279ft)	Descent	0m(0ft)

■ **1** Start by leaving the car park entrance. Turn left along the A591. Pass the Police and Fire Station on the left.

■ **2** Turn left down Stoney Lane cul-de-sac at a footpath sign to Miller Bridge.

■ **3** Turn right at the end of Stoney Lane at a footpath sign with Stock Ghyll on the left. Pass through a kissing-gate. Continue ahead (SW) to go through a wicket-gate. Ahead pass through another wicket-gate. Proceed over the hump-backed Miller Bridge over the River Rothay.

■ **4** Turn right on a minor road (NW) and pass over a cattle-grid adjacent to a field-gate. Stay on this quiet road for 1.2 miles, following the course of the River Rothay on the right. Towards the end of the road, pass over two cattle-grids adjacent to field-gates. Arrive at Peter Bridge.

■ **5** Do not cross the bridge. Turn left (W) onto a tarmac lane with the river on the right. Pass Pelter Bridge car park on the left.

■ **6** Turn right (NNE) at a footpath sign with two cottages on the left at Cote How. Pass through a wicket-gate. Descend a stepped path through trees. Pass through a kissing-gate. Go down a grassy bank. Filter left (W) at a footpath junction. The path winds over grassland with the river to the right.

■ **7** Pass through a kissing-gate. Go through woodland. Emerge through another kissing-gate.

■ **8** Immediately fork left (SW) up a grassy bankside away from the lake. Pass over cross-paths. Filter right onto a broad path at the top of the rise. Cross a footbridge. Bend right along a wall on the right, passing caves on the left. Bend left, uphill, to arrive at Rydal Cave.

SECTION B	2 miles (3.2km)		
Destination	Loughrigg Tarn (GR 345045)		
Ascent	33m(108ft)	Descent	61m(200ft)

■ **9** Turn right up a short rise with a slaty plateau on the right. Proceed for 130m.

■ **10** Go ahead at a major fork (W) along the middle of three paths. Continue to contour round the fell on a terraced path. Keep high, ignoring any branch paths. Climb gradually to the top of a grassy shoulder overlooking Grasmere below on the right.

■ **11** Turn right down the grassy shoulder.

■ **12** Turn left at cross-paths at the bottom of the slope on a col. Proceed along Loughrigg Terrace (WSW) with Grasmere below on the right.

■ **13** Cross a footbridge. Pass through a kissing-gate adjacent to a field-gate. Continue ahead through trees, bearing round left (S), ignoring any right forks. Emerge onto Red Bank Road through a field-gate at a junction.

■ **14** Turn left (SSE) down the road. Proceed for

450m, passing two cottages on the left.

■ **15** Turn left through a kissing-gate adjacent to a field-gate between two stone pillars. Proceed (SE) along a driveway for 600m to a house, The How, on the left above Loughrigg Tarn.

SECTION C	0.8 miles (1.3km)		
Destination	Loughrigg Fell (GR 356043)		
Ascent	92m(302ft)	Descent	0m(0ft)

■ **16** Turn right through a field-gate. Bear left (SE) across meadowland, following a path for 230m. Cross a stile in a metal railed fence to rejoin the driveway. Turn right and proceed for 15m.

■ **17** Turn left over a stile in another metal railed fence. The path ahead gradually climbs a grassy bank and bends right (SSE). Pass over a stile. Continue ahead with woodland to the left and grassland to the right. Pass through a field-gate.

■ **18** Bear left (NE), up a rough stony track. Bend left along a high wall on the right with a wall sign to Ambleside. Follow the wall round to the right to pass through a field-gate with another wall sign to Ambleside. Continue ahead (ESE), climbing gradually, along the wall on the right as far as a sheepfold over the wall on the right.

■ **19** Take the left fork up a narrow loop path (NE), temporarily leaving the wall. Proceed for 250m to rejoin the main path at the wall corner.

■ **20** Go straight ahead on open fell, leaving the wall. The stony path gradually ascends a slope. Bear right at a fork. The path swings left, uphill, to pass over a grassy plateau. Descend to ford a rivulet.

SECTION D	2 miles (3.2km)		
Destination	Ambleside (GR 376047)		
Ascent	44m(144ft)	Descent	193m(633ft)

■ **21** Bear right at a fork on a grassy path. Fork right after 25m. Go up a broad grassy path (ESE) through bracken. Ascend to the top of a rocky outcrop.

■ **22** Turn left from the summit down a narrow path to pass a small tarn on the right. Go to the top of the next rocky outcrop. Turn right, downhill, to pass through a kissing-gate. Continue (ESE) up a broad grassy path for 20m.

■ **23** Fork right through a wall gap. Go uphill to a cairn. Continue down a slope (SE) through a wall gap. Turn right through another wall gap. Keep to the perimeter of the fell, bending left to pass through another wall gap.

■ **24** Turn left (NE). Ascend over a short, steep rocky outcrop. Keep ahead dropping down to cross over a ladder-stile to the left.

■ **25** Go ahead down a slope, bending left (N) along the edge of the fell overlooking Ambleside. Pass a cairn. Bend right (NE) downhill alongside a rivulet. Pass through a stile at the bottom. Proceed through trees to cross a stepped stile.

■ **26** Turn right down a tarmac track. Cross a cattle-grid. Turn right onto a minor road. Cross another cattle-grid to turn left over Miller Bridge at (4). Follow the outward route to the car park.

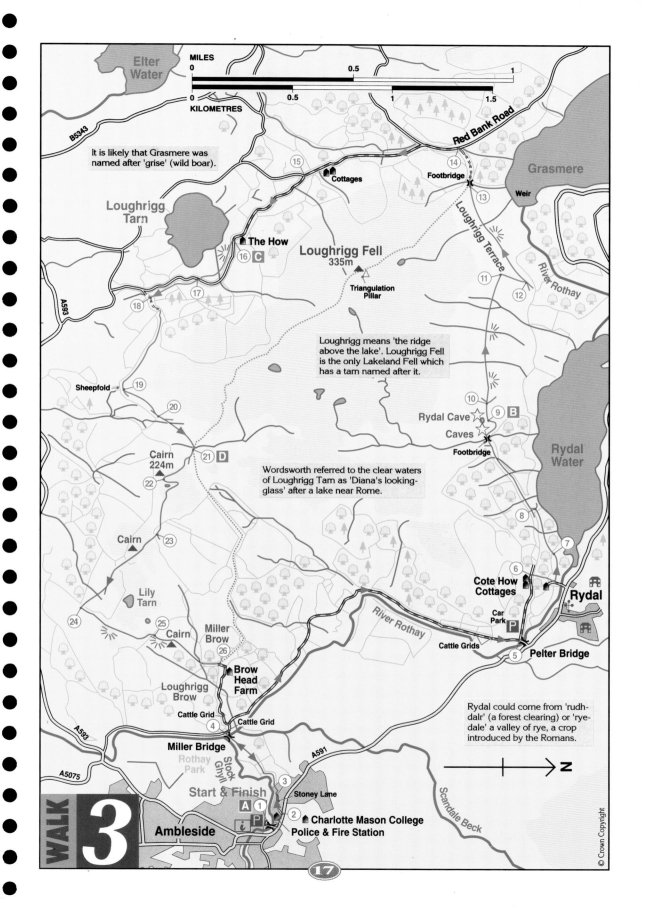

MILES

KILOMETRES

It is likely that Grasmere was named after 'grise' (wild boar).

Red Bank Road

Elter Water

B5343

A593

Loughrigg Tarn

Cottages

15

Footbridge

14

13

Weir

Grasmere

The How

16 C

18

17

Loughrigg Fell
335m

Triangulation Pillar

Loughrigg Terrace

11

12

River Rothay

Loughrigg means 'the ridge above the lake'. Loughrigg Fell is the only Lakeland Fell which has a tarn named after it.

Sheepfold

19

20

10

Rydal Cave

Caves

9 B

Footbridge

Rydal Water

Cairn
224m

21 D

22

Wordsworth referred to the clear waters of Loughrigg Tarn as 'Diana's looking-glass' after a lake near Rome.

8

Cairn

23

7

Lily Tarn

24

25

Cairn

Miller Brow

26

River Rothay

Cote How Cottages

6

Rydal

Car Park
P

Cattle Grids

5

Pelter Bridge

Loughrigg Brow

Brow Head Farm

Cattle Grid

Cattle Grid

4

Miller Bridge

A593

Rothay Park

Stock Ghyll

A591

Rydal could come from 'rudh-dalr' (a forest clearing) or 'rye-dale' a valley of rye, a crop introduced by the Romans.

N

A5075

Start & Finish

Stoney Lane

3

Scandale Beck

WALK

3

Ambleside

A 1

i P

2

Charlotte Mason College
Police & Fire Station

© Crown Copyright

© Crown Copyright

WALK 4

SILVER HOW-
BLEA RIGG-
SERGEANT MAN-
CODALE TARN-
EASEDALE TARN
10 miles (16.1km)

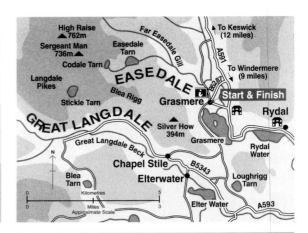

Route Details

Distance	10 miles (16.1km)
Degree of Difficulty	Moderate/Strenuous
Ascent	691m (2,266ft)
Time	7.5 hours

Start and Finish Points

Red Bank car park (GR 337074) in Grasmere village.

From Keswick, take the A591 (S) towards Windermere and turn right onto the B5287 into Grasmere village.

From Windermere, take the A591 (N) towards Keswick. Drive through Ambleside and turn left onto the B5287 into Grasmere village.

The car park is on the left, just past the Information Centre and Nurseries on the minor Red Bank lakeside road towards Skelwith Bridge and Elterwater.

Maps Needed

OS Outdoor Leisure No 7 (1:25 000)
OS Outdoor Leisure No 6 (1:25 000)
OS Landranger No 90 (1:50 000)

Parking Facilities

Red Bank Road pay and display car park in Grasmere village is adjacent to the Lake District National Park Information Centre. There are other car parks at (GR 339073) and (GR 338077).

Short Cuts

At (11) turn right. Descend (E) to join the return route at (16). Omit Codale Tarn by this route in bad weather.

Route Summary

William Wordsworth likened the geographical structure of the Lake District to a wheel, the lakes radiating out like spokes. Its hub, the summit of Sergeant Man, is attained by a scenic path which twists and turns over the long broad ridge of Blea Rigg from the delightful peak of Silver How. Some of the joy of this walk lies in following the capricious meanderings of this path. The only drawback lies in low cloud which can obscure the many criss-cross paths on this broad open ridge, and the walk should not be attempted in mist.

A quiet lane leaves Grasmere en route for Silver How summit

Providing the weather is good, the descent via Codale Tarn is an explorer's delight, encountering a sheltered grassy shelf which harbours one of Lakeland's prettiest and most secluded tarns. Leaving the deserted shores of Codale Tarn for the more populated banks of Easedale Tarn provides entrance to a realm of cascading waterfalls and fine mountain scenery. It is easy to imagine why one of Lakeland's deepest tarns in this idyllic setting served as a literary inspiration to William Wordsworth and his sister Dorothy. Equally enchanting is the descent alongside the tumbling falls of Sourmilk Gill.

Interesting Features

LANDFORMS Rising from the junction of the Rothay and Brathay Rivers at Ambleside (SE) is Loughrigg Fell. From there, a wide broken ridge extends for 5.5 miles, passing over the pinnacle of Silver How, dividing en route Langdale (W) and Easedale (E), and continuing over Sergeant Man to High Raise (NW). The ridge is an undulating plateau which only narrows as it climbs over Blea Rigg.

The rocky summit of Sergeant Man is the geographical centre of the Lakeland Fells. It lies (S) of a broad expanse, dropping down from High Raise and continues (S) to the Stickle Tarn basin.

The descent from Sergeant Man, via Codale and Easedale Tarns, sitting in their hanging valleys, encounters rock pinnacles, splintered fissures, and tumbling waterfalls, all characteristics of the Borrowdale volcanic mountain structure. Easedale Tarn has a maximum depth of 21 metres (69ft), making it one of Lakeland's deepest tarns.

HISTORY Towards the end of the walk, a visit to the C13th St Oswald's Church is worthwhile. Inside is a memorial to William Wordsworth. In the churchyard is his grave, and those of other members of the family. Until 1881, the church floor was earthen and rushes were laid to keep it warm and dry. The ancient rush-bearing ceremony still survives, enacted annually in a procession by village children on the Saturday nearest August 5th. The girls wear crowns of flowers, the boys carry rushes, and they are rewarded with a piece of traditional gingerbread.

VIEWPOINTS Silver How lives up to its lovely name as a viewpoint. (E) is a rich picture of the vale, village and lake of Grasmere, as well as Rydal Water, above which Nab Scar marks the start of a long ridge climbing (N) to the summit of Fairfield. (N) above the village is Helm Crag with its distinctive rock configuration, locally known as 'The Lion and the Lamb' and 'The Lady at the Organ'. Beyond, on the skyline, is the summit of Blencathra, to the right of which the eye travels round the peaks of the Helvellyn range to Fairfield. (E) lie the distant Kentmere Fells, and to the right Wansfell Pike occupies the middle distance, whilst (SE) in the foreground is Loughrigg Fell and Tarn with the upper reaches of Windermere beyond. (S) can be glimpsed a small part of Coniston Water, with Wetherlam and Swirl How above to the right. (WSW) is Pike of Blisco, Crinkle Crags and Bow Fell. (W) the Langdale Pikes are very prominent. (NW) is the summit of Sergeant Man.

Descending from Silver How are slate quarries (S) with Elter Water beyond Elterwater village.

From (9) is a dramatic view (E) down to Easedale Tarn with Codale Tarn on a shelf above to the left. From (10) Stickle Tarn can be seen (W) beneath a curving ridge from Harrison Stickle to the sheer rock wall of Pavey Ark.

The tumbling cataracts of Sourmilk Gill below Easedale Tarn

The most striking view from Sergeant Man is (S), where Pavey Ark and Harrison Stickle rise from Stickle Tarn against a distant backdrop of Coniston fells. (SW) are Crinkle Crags, Bow Fell and the Scafells; (NW) the dull slope up to High Raise; (N) Skiddaw and Blencathra; and (NE) from left to right the Helvellyn, Fairfield and High Street ranges. (SE) can be discerned Elter Water, Rydal Water, Esthwaite Water and beyond to Windermere.

From the bank above Easedale Tarn's eastern outlet stream (NW) across Easedale is a long ridge which terminates in the craggy summit of Helm Crag. Beyond, below Fairfield, is the rounded dome of Seat Sandal which serves as a local barometer, a grey cap indicating that rain is on the way. Similarly the Wordsworths called Easedale 'the black quarter' from where bad weather comes.

Cross-Section of the Route

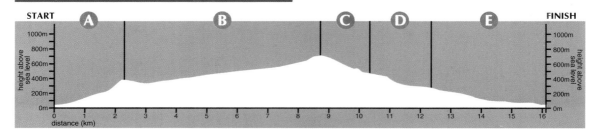

Route Description

SECTION A	1.5 miles (2.4km)		
Destination	Silver How (GR 327066)		
Ascent	330m(1082ft)	Descent	0m(0ft)

■ **1** Start from the car park entrance. Turn left on the minor Red Bank Road.

■ **2** Turn right, off the road, at a footpath sign with a boating-hut and landing-stages on the left and the entrance to Kelbarrow House on the right. Pass through a field-gate. Go ahead (W) up a broad walled track. Pass through a kissing-gate. Follow a wall on the left. Continue (W) uphill over grassland at the wall corner on the left.

■ **3** Pass through a kissing-gate. Go ahead, bending left (SW) uphill with a wall on the left. Pass through a kissing-gate. Ford a rivulet. Proceed uphill (SSW) with the wall on the left.

■ **4** Double back right at the top of the rise at a small cairn on cross-paths. Ascend a steep gully (NW) up a grassy path which becomes a scree path. Pass a cairn. Bend left at a cairn at the top. Bend left again after 80m up a twisting path onto the summit of Silver How (395m/1,296ft).

SECTION B	4 miles (6.4km)		
Destination	Sergeant Man (GR 286089)		
Ascent	361m(1184ft)	Descent	20m(65ft)

■ **5** Turn right (SSW) from the summit cairn on an undulating grassy ridge path, making for a large cairn in the distance. Pass the cairn. Pass a smaller cairn 25m ahead. Continue ahead downhill.

■ **6** Turn right (W) at a narrow grassy plateau onto a broad path. Fork right (NW) after 80m. Follow (N) a gradually ascending thin grassy path with Megs Gill below on the left.

■ **7** Double back left (W) after a small tarn at a junction. Go along a broad twisting path which ascends (WNW) gradually, passing two small tarns and a larger tarn on the left. The path bends right (NW) below Lang How on the right, then left (W), then right (NW). At the top of the rise descend over the boggy depression of Swinscar Hause.

■ **8** Bear right, ascending (NNW) on a cairned path over Little Castle How. When it bends sharply left, proceed for 15m, then turn sharply right. Ascend with a short rock wall on the left. Continue uphill (NW), bending left (W) below Great Castle How up on the right, passing two small tarns on the left. Bend sharply right (N) up to a viewpoint over Easedale Tarn far below.

■ **9** Bend left (W) below Blea Crag up on the right. Follow ahead over Blea Rigg plateau.

■ **10** Bear right (NW) at a pointed cairn with Stickle Tarn below on the left. Follow an indistinct path, later cairned, up a humpy ridge with Codale Tarn and Easedale Tarn in view, below on the right.

■ **11** Continue ahead, uphill, at a right junction.

■ **12** Bend left (NNW) at an unmarked right junction with a wide flat upward sloping rock slab on the left. The ascending path bends right, then left to ford a shallow rivulet. Climb a short rocky stairway (W) to the summit of Sergeant Man (736m/2,414ft).

SECTION C	1 mile (1.6km)		
Destination	Codale Tarn (GR 297089)		
Ascent	0m(0ft)	Descent	261m(856ft)

■ **13** From the summit cairn retrace the outward route to (12). Bear left, off the ridge, at the unmarked junction. Descend a sloping grassy shelf on an indistinct path (ENE), keeping along the foot of rocky outcrops on the left for 250m.

■ **14** Turn right at a large outcrop of jagged rock. Go down a grassy slope (SSE) with a reeded rivulet on the right. Bear left (NE) after 130m, below a hummock, away from the rivulet. Descend a grassy slope, to join the northern point of Codale Tarn.

SECTION D	1.3 miles (2.2km)		
Destination	Easedale Tarn (GR 310087)		
Ascent	0m(0ft)	Descent	185m(607ft)

■ **15** Ford a shallow inlet brook. Bend right on a path, skirting the eastern shore of the tarn to ford the outlet stream. At the southern end of the tarn, the path bends left (SSE) round the foot of Belles Knott up on the left to ford another shallow rivulet.

■ **16** Turn left (E) at a junction onto a rocky twisting downhill path with waterfalls descending on the left. At the bottom, the undulating path (E) bends left (ENE) with Easedale Tarn below on the left.

SECTION E	2.2 miles (3.5km)		
Destination	Grasmere (GR 337074)		
Ascent	0m(0ft)	Descent	225m(738ft)

■ **17** Bend right on a bridleway at the foot of the tarn, descending (E) with Sourmilk Gill on the left. The path bends right, passing waterfalls on the left.

■ **18** Cross a footbridge over Little Brinhowe Gill to join a wall on the left. Pass over a stone-slab footbridge to join a wall on the right. Go through a kissing-gate at the bottom of the slope. Continue ahead through a field-gate. The path bends right with Brimmer Head Farm away on the left.

■ **19** Go over a concrete footbridge at cross-paths. Pass through the left of two adjacent metal field-gates at a wall sign on the left to Grasmere. Continue ahead (ESE) on a path along Easedale Beck on the left to emerge onto open grassland.

■ **20** Pass through a metal field-gate. Go ahead through trees over a stone-slab footbridge to cross a larger stepped footbridge. Emerge onto the minor Easedale Road.

■ **21** Turn right down the road. Cross Goody Bridge to emerge at the B5287 junction in Grasmere.

■ **22** Go straight across with shops on the left and a small car park on the right. Filter left at another junction with the B5287. Turn sharp right across the road with the church ahead. Go up Red Bank Road. Pass the Information Centre on the left. Turn left into the car park.

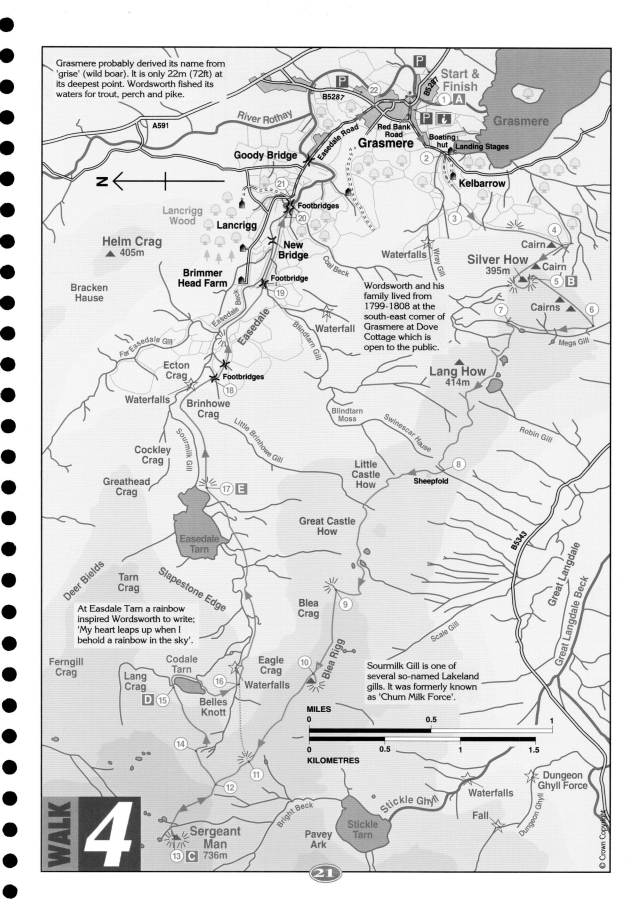

Grasmere probably derived its name from 'grise' (wild boar). It is only 22m (72ft) at its deepest point. Wordsworth fished its waters for trout, perch and pike.

Wordsworth and his family lived from 1799-1808 at the south-east corner of Grasmere at Dove Cottage which is open to the public.

At Easdale Tarn a rainbow inspired Wordsworth to write; 'My heart leaps up when I behold a rainbow in the sky'.

Sourmilk Gill is one of several so-named Lakeland gills. It was formerly known as 'Churn Milk Force'.

River Rothay
A591
A591
B5287
Goody Bridge
Easedale Road
Red Bank Road
Grasmere
Boating hut
Landing Stages
Start & Finish
Grasmere
Kelbarrow
Lancrigg Wood
Lancrigg
Footbridges
New Bridge
Waterfalls
Wray Gill
Silver How 395m
Cairn
Cairn
Cairns
Helm Crag
▲ 405m
Brimmer Head Farm
Footbridge
Coal Beck
Bracken Hause
Easedale Beck
Easedale
Blindtarn Gill
Waterfall
Megs Gill
Ecton Crag
Footbridges
Far Easedale Gill
Waterfalls
Brinhowe Crag
Little Brinhowe Gill
Lang How 414m
Blindtarn Moss
Swinescar Hause
Robin Gill
Cockley Crag
Sourmilk Gill
Greathead Crag
Little Castle How
Sheepfold
Easedale Tarn
Great Castle How
B5343
Deer Bields
Tarn Crag
Slapestone Edge
Scale Gill
Great Langdale
Great Langdale Beck
Blea Crag
Ferngill Crag
Codale Tarn
Lang Crag
Eagle Crag Waterfalls
Blea Rigg
Belles Knott

MILES
0   0.5   1

KILOMETRES
0   0.5   1   1.5

Bright Beck
Stickle Ghyll
Dungeon Ghyll Force
Waterfalls
Fall
Stickle Tarn
Pavey Ark
Sergeant Man
736m
Dungeon Ghyll

© Crown Copyright

WALK 4

21

© Crown Copyright

WALK 5

GRASMERE-STEEL FELL-CALF CRAG-GIBSON KNOTT-HELM CRAG

8.7 miles (14km)

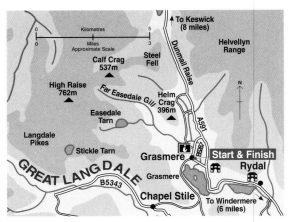

Route Details

Distance	8.7 miles (14km)
Degree of Difficulty	Moderate
Ascent	662m (2,171ft)
Time	6.5 hours

Start and Finish Points

Broadgate Meadow car park (GR 338077) in Grasmere village.

From Keswick, take the A591 (S) towards Windermere, to Grasmere village and turn right before the Swan Hotel on the left.

From Windermere, take the A591 (N) towards Keswick, through Ambleside, continuing to the second turning on the left into Grasmere at the Swan Hotel on the right.

Go down the B5287 towards the village centre. Turn left into the car park at Grasmere Hall on the left.

Maps Needed

OS Outdoor Leisure No 7 (1:25 000)
OS Outdoor Leisure No 4 (1:25 000)
OS Landranger No 90 (1:50 000)

Parking Facilities

Broadgate Meadow pay and display car park. Other car parks are at (GR 339073) and (GR 337074).

Short Cuts

At (14), turn left down the fell, bending right (E). Follow a twisting downhill path. Turn left to find Green Burn. Turn right (ESE) with Green Burn on the right. Emerge at (7) to retrace the outward route to the car park.

Route Summary

The early part of this popular route from Grasmere follows a leafy lane bordering the River Rothay, ascending a delightful valley. The gradual climb over springy turf up the southern ridge of Steel Fell opens out backward views over the Greenburn Valley and up to the multi-shaped crags which top the ridge containing Helm Crag.

The placid water of Grasmere shimmers in the afternoon sun

The route from Steel Fell to Calf Crag is often boggy underfoot. Another ridge is soon attained, along whose length there are superb views of the Easedale Valley nestling below. At its end lies Helm Crag. Its eminent position and significant shape when viewed from Grasmere below has earned it the affectionate name of 'The Lion and the Lamb'. From below it invites exploration. Once atop its summit it lives up to the invitation, its crags evoking the experience of real mountaineering whilst exuding natural charm and serenity. The picture over the Vale of Grasmere, backed with the rugged outline of the Langdale Pikes, provides one of those Lakeland scenes long-etched in the memory. It requires an effort of will to tear oneself away from such an enchanting vista into the real world below.

Interesting Features

LANDFORMS The craggy sides of Steel Fell rise from a triangular base. Green Burn (W) and the River Rothay (E), both describe sinuous courses in their higher reaches between hummocks of glacial moraine left behind when the ice receded from these deep glaciated valleys. The deep trough of the Wythburn Valley (N) contains Thirlmere. (W) over the head of the Greenburn Valley is Steel Fell's only link with the other fells.

Calf Crag lies at the end of a long ridge which curves (E) to Helm Crag. Its extreme (N) boundary stretches in easy gradients over marshy ground down to Wyth Burn. Craggy shelves form the steep flanks which drop into the Greenburn valley (N) and Far Easdale (S).

At the centre of the serrated ridge lies Gibson Knott before encountering Helm Crag, the jewel in the crown. On the Helm Crag summit, 250 metres in length, natural convulsions have created a craggy fortress with rock towers at either end. Their distinctive configuration, viewed from below, have earned these towers a variety of popular names: 'The Lion and the Lamb', or 'The Lion Couchant', or 'The Old Woman Playing the Organ', or 'The Howitzer'. These shapes are not clear from close proximity, though the tangle of crags make the summit of this midget mountain more dramatic than even Scafell Pike.

HISTORY Thirlmere, seen (N) from the summit of Steel Fell, provides water for the urban areas of south Lancashire, nearly 100 miles away. It was acquired by Manchester Corporation in 1879 only after strong local opposition, including that of John Ruskin who wrote to 'The Times' in 1877 that 'Manchester is plotting to steal the waters of Thirlmere and the clouds of Helvellyn'. To raise the water level 16m (54ft) necessitated the merging of two small lakes and drowning the village of Wythburn and its farmsteads.

Easedale Tarn is one of Lakeland's deepest tarns. It was here that a rainbow inspired Wordsworth to compose the oft-quoted lines:

'My heart leaps up when I behold
A rainbow in the sky'.

On 'The Poets Walk' through Lancrigg Wood is a stone tablet with a Latin inscription by Dorothy Wordsworth in praise of her brother. As William recited lines on their walks, his sister copied them into a notebook.

St Oswald's Church, Grasmere, Wordsworth's final resting-place

VIEWPOINTS (N), from the summit of Steel Fell is Thirlmere below, with the solid fortress of Blencathra providing a fitting background. (W) Great Gable and Glaramara can be discerned, and (SW) the serrated skyline of the Coniston fells. Lakes in evidence are Thirlmere (N), two sections of Grasmere and Esthwaite Water (SSE), and two sections of Windermere (SE).

From Calf Crag (SE), is the contrasting landscape scenery down the glaciated valley of Far Easdale, leading into the Vale of Grasmere with its lake, a small part of Rydal Water beyond that, and the middle reaches of Windermere in the distance.

Not having the advantage of great height, Helm Crag cannot command views over the high fells, but pride of place must go to a classic Lakeland view (SE) over the beautiful Vale of Grasmere and its lake, with the upper reaches of Windermere and Esthwaite Water beyond. (SW) the distinctive shape of the Langdale Pikes are silhouetted against the skyline. (WSW) is the view of Easedale Tarn nestled beneath Tarn Crag. (E) is a long summit ridge crowned by Fairfield (NE), fronted by the rounded dome of Seat Sandal which serves as a local barometer, a grey cap indicating that rain is on the way.

Cross-Section of the Route

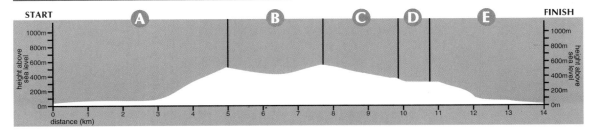

Route Description

SECTION A	3.2 miles (5.1km)		
Destination	Steel Fell (GR 319112)		
Ascent	488m(1601ft)	Descent	0m(0ft)

■ **1** Start from the car park entrance. Cross the B5287. Turn right on a pathway (N) alongside the road on the right.

■ **2** Turn left just before the road bridge at a footpath sign. Go through a kissing-gate. Proceed (W), bending left, uphill, through trees with the River Rothay below on the right.

■ **3** Turn right (NW) through a field-gate. Go along the Easedale Road to cross Goody Bridge over Easedale Beck. Proceed for 65m.

■ **4** Turn right down a minor road. For 0.8 miles follow the valley road (N) parallel to the River Rothay down on the right.

■ **5** Bear left at the road junction with Low Mill Bridge on the right. Cross a humpback bridge.

■ **6** Immediately take the left fork (NW) on an ascending driveway. After 120m, go through a metal wicket-gate adjacent to a cattle-grid. Continue ahead for 30m through a metal kissing-gate adjacent to another cattle-grid. Keep ahead, bending left, passing two cottages on the right at Helmside. Go through a field-gate at the end of the driveway, onto grassland with a sign to Greenburn.

■ **7** Turn sharp right (NW) at a junction. Follow the wall on the right up a grassy path for 250m. Pass through a wall gap at a corner. Go through a field-gate after another 150m where walls meet.

■ **8** Bear left, to continue up the ridge (NW). After 100m, proceed along a wall on the left to pass through a field-gate.

■ **9** Continue ahead uphill (NW). At a rocky outcrop, bend right, then left to pass round it on a narrow ascending ledge path. At the top, go ahead over Cotra Breast to another high point on the ridge. The grassy path now bears round left, rising gradually (NW) to the summit cairn of Steel Fell (553m/1,814ft) at Dead Pike.

SECTION B	1.7 miles (2.7km)		
Destination	Calf Crag (GR 302104)		
Ascent	69m(226ft)	Descent	85m(278ft)

■ **10** From the summit cairn, go ahead (WNW), along a fence on the right. The path bends left to a fence corner on the right. Continue ahead (W) just below the ridge on the the right and intermittent iron fence posts. The path descends (WSW) into a depression with small tarns to the left and right.

■ **11** With one of the larger tarns on the right, the path gradually curves left to cross over marshy ground. As it begins to climb (SW), follow a line of intermittent iron fence-posts on the right.

■ **12** Turn sharp left (E) at the top of the rise, away from the fence corner, with a large iron fence-post with metal supports on the right and a small tarn below on the right. Ascend onto the ridge to the summit cairn of Calf Crag (537m/1,761ft).

SECTION C	1.2 miles (2km)		
Destination	Gibson Knott (GR 322099)		
Ascent	20m(66ft)	Descent	137m(450ft)

■ **13** Continue ahead from the cairn, descending with the ridge up on the left. The path bends right over peat hags, then left to pass the rocky outcrop of Pike of Carrs on the right. Go ahead for 200m.

■ **14** At a footpath junction, to the left, continue ahead. The undulating path meanders (ESE) below the ridge on to the summit cairn of Gibson Knott (420m/1,378ft).

SECTION D	0.6 miles (1km)		
Destination	Helm Crag (GR 327093)		
Ascent	85m(278ft)	Descent	100m(328ft)

■ **15** Continue ahead on the ridge from the cairn. Descend (SE) to cross the grassy saddle of Bracken Hause. The path now zig-zags steeply uphill to the north-west summit of Helm Crag (405m/1,328ft).

SECTION E	2 miles (3.2km)		
Destination	Grasmere (GR 338077)		
Ascent	0m(0ft)	Descent	340m(1115ft)

■ **16** Continue along the summit ridge (S) for 250m to another craggy outcrop on the left. Descend quite steeply ahead towards Grasmere. At a grassy saddle curve right (W) at a low cairn. Descend a shaly path which bends left (SE) over White Crag.

■ **17** Turn right (SW) at a wall corner. Follow a stepped path downhill, along the wall on the left. Bend right where the wall ends. Go along a wooden fence on the left. The path bends left, then right to join a wall on the left. Continue for 50m.

■ **18** Turn left down a stony lane between walls. Turn left at a footpath sign to Grasmere after 100m. Turn right, through a metal field-gate, after 60m.

■ **19** Immediately turn left, up some steps, at a permissive footpath sign to the Wordsworth Memorial. Pass through a kissing-gate into Lancrigg Wood. Continue ahead (E) between wire fences for 100m. Go up stone steps through a wall gap. Bend round a former pond on the right to take a left waymarked fork.

■ **20** Pass the Wordsworth Memorial, on the left, to go through a wicket-gate. Ahead, pass between farm buildings. Bend right, behind Lancrigg House. Filter onto a lane at the house entrance on the right. Go through a metal wicket-gate adjacent to a cattle-grid. Continue ahead (S) over cross-tracks down the lane.

■ **21** Filter left onto Easedale Road at the end of the drive. Continue along the road (SE) passing (4) and (3) to the junction with the B5287 in Grasmere .

■ **22** Turn left, on the pathway, along the road on the right. Continue for 150m.

■ **23** At Grasmere Hall, adjacent to the Grasmere Hotel over the road, turn right to cross the road into the car park.

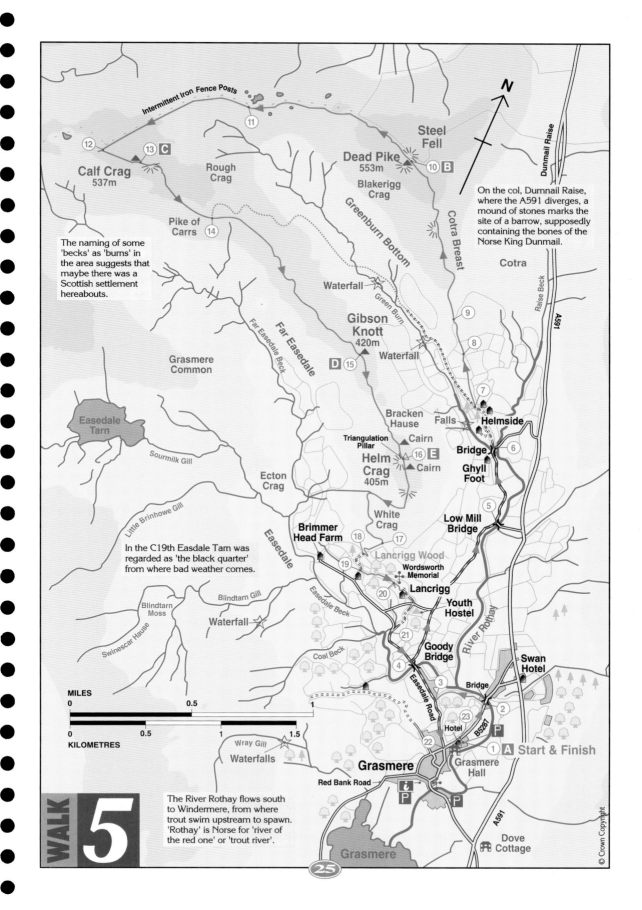

N

Intermittent Iron Fence Posts

⑪

Steel
Fell

⑫ ⑬ C

Calf Crag
537m

Rough
Crag

Dead Pike
553m ⑩ B

Blakerigg
Crag

Dunmail Raise

On the col, Dumnail Raise,
where the A591 diverges, a
mound of stones marks the
site of a barrow, supposedly
containing the bones of the
Norse King Dunmail.

Cotra

Pike of
Carrs ⑭

The naming of some
'becks' as 'burns' in
the area suggests that
maybe there was a
Scottish settlement
hereabouts.

Greenburn Bottom

Cotra Breast

Waterfall

Green Burn

⑨

⑧

Gibson
Knott
420m

Far Easedale

Far Easedale Beck

Grasmere
Common

Waterfall

D ⑮

Raise Beck

A591

Bracken
Hause

Falls

⑦

Helmside

Easedale
Tarn

Sourmilk Gill

Triangulation
Pillar

Cairn

⑯ E

Cairn

Bridge

Ghyll
Foot

⑥

Helm
Crag
405m

Ecton
Crag

Little Brinhowe Gill

White
Crag

Low Mill
Bridge

⑤

In the C19th Easedale Tarn was
regarded as 'the black quarter'
from where bad weather comes.

Easedale

Brimmer
Head Farm

⑱

⑰

Lancrigg Wood

Wordsworth
Memorial

Lancrigg

River Rothay

⑲

⑳

Blindtarn Gill

Youth
Hostel

Blindtarn
Moss

Easedale Beck

Swinescar Hause

Waterfall

Coal Beck

㉑

Goody
Bridge

④

Swan
Hotel

③

Bridge

MILES
0   0.5   1

0   0.5   1   1.5
KILOMETRES

Easedale Road

④

㉓

Hotel

②

B5287

P

Wray Gill

Waterfalls

㉒

① A Start & Finish

Grasmere

Red Bank Road

Grasmere
Hall

i
P

P

The River Rothay flows south
to Windermere, from where
trout swim upstream to spawn.
'Rothay' is Norse for 'river of
the red one' or 'trout river'.

Grasmere

Dove
Cottage

© Crown Copyright

WALK 5

© Crown Copyright

WALK 6

LOFT CRAG-PIKE OF STICKLE-HARRISON STICKLE-PAVEY ARK-STICKLE TARN

5.1 miles (8.2km)

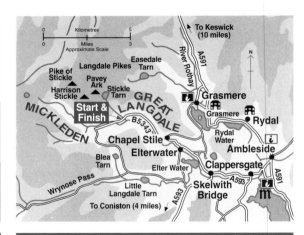

Route Details

Distance	5.1 miles (8.2km)
Degree of Difficulty	Moderate/Strenuous
Ascent	816m (2,677ft)
Time	5 hours

Start and Finish Points

Stickle Ghyll National Trust car park (GR 295064).

From Ambleside follow the A593 (SW) from Ambleside. Continue through Clappersgate (W). Take the right fork on approaching Skelwith Bridge on the B5343 by-passing Elterwater and through Chapel Stile, (NW) up Great Langdale.

Maps Needed

OS Outdoor Leisure No 6 (1:25 000)
OS Landranger No 90 (1:50 000)

Parking Facilities

There is a smaller car park (GR 296064) on the left of the B5343, 100 metres before the Stickle Ghyll car park on the right. Both car parks are close to the Sticklebarn public bar and the New Dungeon Ghyll Hotel.

Short Cuts

At (20) turn left with Stickle Ghyll on the right. Scramble down right to the gill after 200 metres. Keep Stickle Ghyll on the right, descending an engineered stone path.

Pass through a wall gap on the lower slopes. Cross a stile. Turn right over a footbridge. Turn left with the gill on the left. Descend to (3). Follow the outward route to (1).

Route Summary

Viewed at a distance, the distinctive outline of the Langdale Pikes registers an irresistible appeal. On closer inspection, the peaks are even more impressive as they soar abruptly skywards from the broad pastureland of Great Langdale. It is hard to believe that the five closely compacted summits are below 762 metres (2,500ft) and can be scaled over such a short distance. Part of the excitement of the expedition is the ease with which these heights can be attained. However, the ascent and descent of rugged volcanic slopes takes longer than expected, even though the paths are good throughout.

Langdale Pikes etched into the skyline from Great Langdale

The rewards are undeniable; superb distant views from airy ridges of surrounding mountains, valleys, lakes and tarns; magnificent close-ups of craggy cliffs, buttresses, scree gullies and ravines; a glimpse of a Stone Age industrial site; and Stickle Tarn, set beneath a colossal precipice. Each summit above craggy slopes invites periods of quiet contemplation of vistas from grassy couches and bilberry terraces. Equally exciting is the high level descent from Stickle Tarn via Pike Howe, or straight down Stickle Ghyll alongside a series of cataracts.

Interesting Features

LANDFORMS The Langdale Pikes (Pike of Stickle, Harrison Stickle, Loft Crag, Thorn Crag and Pavey Ark) rise abruptly from a broad base in Great Langdale. The most southerly, Loft Crag, has its summit above the massive buttress of Gimmer Crag and is separated from its subsidiary summit of Thorn Crag (E) by the deep ravine of Dungeon Ghyll. A precipitous wall of crags dropping into the Mickleden valley forms its south-western flank and leads (NW) via a lofty ridge to the summit of Pike of Stickle which literally sticks out like a sore thumb. This thimble-shaped rounded summit affords a dramatic prospect over its western edge down Stickle Breast, an almost sheer rock wall bounded by scree gullies, which drops 610 metres (2,000ft) into the Mickleden valley. Its northern and eastern flanks are less dramatic, as they fall away into the upland hollow of Harrison Combe which gradually descends (N) over the plateau of Martcrag Moor to Stake Pass. Over the upper fringe of the combe (E) is the summit of Harrison Stickle, a lofty narrow ridge, 70 metres in length. Its north-eastern near-perpendicular jagged facade sweeps (NE) in an arc of crags to the summit of Pavey Ark on the eastern edge of Thunacar Knott. A gigantic southern precipice plunges sheer from Pavey Ark into the waters of Stickle Tarn beneath. There is a diagonal gash in this precipice called Jack's Rake which provides a route to and from Stickle Tarn, though it is more of a rock climb than a walk.

HISTORY The head of the wide scree gully, east of Pike of Stickle, marks the site of one of the many Lakeland Stone Age axe 'factories' of Neolithic Man, probably established 4,000 years ago. A chance C20th discovery of a prolific number of axes designated the site as the most important of its kind in the country. Material for axe-heads was supplied by a thin intrusive vein of exceptionally hard volcanic rock. Excessive erosion caused by the attentions of aspiring archaeologists has resulted in a National Trust closure of the gully slope.

VIEWPOINTS The bilberry-covered peak of Loft Crag juts out over Great Langdale, so affording a bird's-eye view along the length of the valley below. Another view of Great Langdale can be captured from the south cairn of Harrison Stickle, and is further enhanced from Pavey Ark.

All the Langdale Pikes afford similar distant views, so each summit is not itemised individually as the general direction from all of them is roughly the same. (N) on the horizon is Skiddaw with Blencathra to its right; (NE) is the Helvellyn range, and moving right St Sunday Crag, then the Fairfield/Nab Scar ridge fronted by the Gibson Knott/Helm Crag ridge. Going round (E) is the skyline of the High Street range and the Kentmere Fells. (ESE) Silver How and Loughrigg Fell occupy the middleground backed by Wansfell Pike. (S) are the Coniston fells, whilst Pike of Blisco across the Mickleden valley is prominent in the foreground. (SW) is the distinctive serrated edge of Crinkle Crags, whilst the Bow Fell pyramid is particularly prominent (WSW). (W) is Scafell Pike with Great End, Great Gable, and Green Gable seen to the right, and High Stile in the further distance. (NW) is the whale-backed summit of Grasmoor, the skyline moving north etched with the peaks of Dale Head, Crag Hill, Grisedale Pike and Causey Pike.

A familiar Lakeland view of the distinctive Langdale Pikes

A variety of tarns can be observed from the summits. (E) the small unnamed tarns between Lang How and Silver How; (ESE) Loughrigg Tarn and Elterwater; (SE) Lingmoor Tarn, Esthwaite Water, Wise Een Tarn, and two sections of Windermere; (SSE) Blea Tarn; and (NNW) Tarn at Leaves on Rosthwaite Fell. The best aerial view of Stickle Tarn is from the summit of Pavey Ark.

Cross-Section of the Route

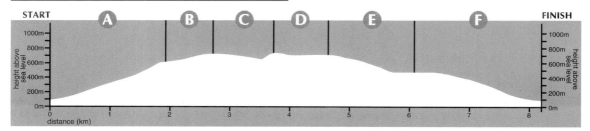

Route Description

SECTION A	1.4 miles (2.2km)	
Destination	Loft Crag (GR 279071)	
Ascent	600m(1968ft) Descent 0m(0ft)	

■ 1 Start at the top of the Stickle Ghyll car park. Turn left in front of the toilets adjacent to the Sticklebarn bar. Go up steps to proceed along a stony path for 15m.

■ 2 Turn right through a wicket-gate. Turn left through a wall gap after another 15m. Follow an uphill path along a wire fence on the left. Turn left between posts in a wire fence.

■ 3 Take the left fork at a junction. The path ascends (W) along a wall on the left. Pass through a kissing-gate adjacent to a field-gate at the top of the rise.

■ 4 Turn right (NW) along a wall on the right. Proceed for 140m. Cross a stile.

■ 5 Turn half-left downhill to ford a stream. Ascend a path between a wall on the left and Dungeon Ghyll on the right. Continue ahead (W) at a wall corner on the left. Proceed up the fell on a stony zig-zagging cairned path for 500m.

■ 6 Turn sharp right at three rock walls and a scree slope ahead. Climb rock steps up Mark Gate gully. Bend sharp left, continuing up the gully. The path bends right (NW) at the top. Continue up a gradual grassy slope to a cairn.

■ 7 Bear left (WNW) on a faint path which soon is cairned. It rises gradually, veering right towards two rounded peaks of Gimmer Crag and Thorn Crag. Ascend a red scree slope ahead (NNW) with Gimmer Crag, a climber's crag, on the left.

■ 8 Turn left on emerging onto a grassy plateau at the top of the scree. Proceed for 200m.

■ 9 Turn sharp left up another scree path, bending right to the summit cairn of Loft Crag (692m/2,270ft).

SECTION B	0.5 miles (0.8km)	
Destination	Pike of Stickle (GR 274073)	
Ascent	60m(197ft)	Descent 43m(140ft)

■ 10 Turn right (NW) from the cairn along a ridge path towards the distinctive rounded peak of Pike of Stickle ahead.

■ 11 Veer left after the second of two depressions, passing a steep scree gully on the left. Ascend a rocky path round the right side of the summit. The path gives way to a minor rock scramble up left to the summit of Pike of Stickle (709m/2,325ft).

SECTION C	0.7 miles (1.1km)	
Destination	Harrison Stickle (GR 282073)	
Ascent	125m(410ft)	Descent 98m(323ft)

■ 12 From Pike of Stickle retrace the route to (11). Take a left fork (E) towards the long summit of Harrison Stickle directly ahead. Cross a marshy plateau (E), skirting to the right to avoid the worst of the soggy patches.

■ 13 Fork right at the edge of the plateau. Follow a path, ascending diagonally right (ESE) with some minor scrambling to the south summit of Harrison Stickle (736m/2,414ft).

SECTION D	0.6 miles (1km)	
Destination	Pavey Ark (GR 286079)	
Ascent	31m(102ft)	Descent 69m(226ft)

■ 14 From the south summit cairn, turn left (N) along the flat summit ridge to the north summit cairn.

■ 15 Bear down left (NNW) from the cairn. Descend over rocks. Turn right (N) on a path at the bottom. Ignore any left forks and keep bearing right.

■ 16 The path bears right (NE) at a fork towards the huge outcrop of rocks of Pavey Ark. Pass three small tarns on the right. Continue ahead past another small tarn on the left. Ascend left round a sharp outcrop of rock. The cairned level path continues gradually bending right, contouring round the fell (ENE) over a boulder-field. Pass through a wall gap to ascend to the summit of Pavey Ark (698m/2,289ft).

SECTION E	0.8 miles (1.3km)	
Destination	Stickle Tarn (GR 287075)	
Ascent	0m(0ft)	Descent 118m(387ft)

■ 17 Retrace the route to the wall gap. Turn right along the wall on the right. Proceed to a cairned junction.

■ 18 Turn right at the cairn. Steeply descend a broad rocky path (E) down a gully with Pavey Ark up on the right. Bear left at a small plateau. Skirt left round a rocky outcrop on the right. The path again descends, bending right.

■ 19 Ford the shallow Bright Beck at the bottom. Turn right (S) on a path over grassy mounds. Keep the beck on the right to arrive at the north-east corner of Stickle Tarn. Bend right across stepping-stones over a rivulet. Follow the path (SSW) round the eastern shore of the tarn.

SECTION F	1.1 miles (1.8km)	
Destination	Stickle Ghyll car park (GR 295064)	
Ascent	0m(0ft)	Descent 488m(1601ft)

■ 20 Go ahead at the south end of the tarn. Ford Stickle Ghyll over large boulders. Ahead, pass over a broad path at the side of a dam wall. Immediately fork left (S) up a grassy path onto a short ridge. Turn right along the ridge (W). Follow a path which contours round the fell.

■ 21 Fork left (SSE) on a stony cairned path, descending a grassy ridge to a depression and onto the summit of Pike Howe.

■ 22 Turn round. Bend left, keeping to the right of an eroded path on a steep engineered stone path. Follow round left (ESE) below the summit of Pike Howe, descending quite steeply to a wall.

■ 23 Turn right. Follow the path down along the wall on the left to (5). Cross the stile and follow the outward route to (1).

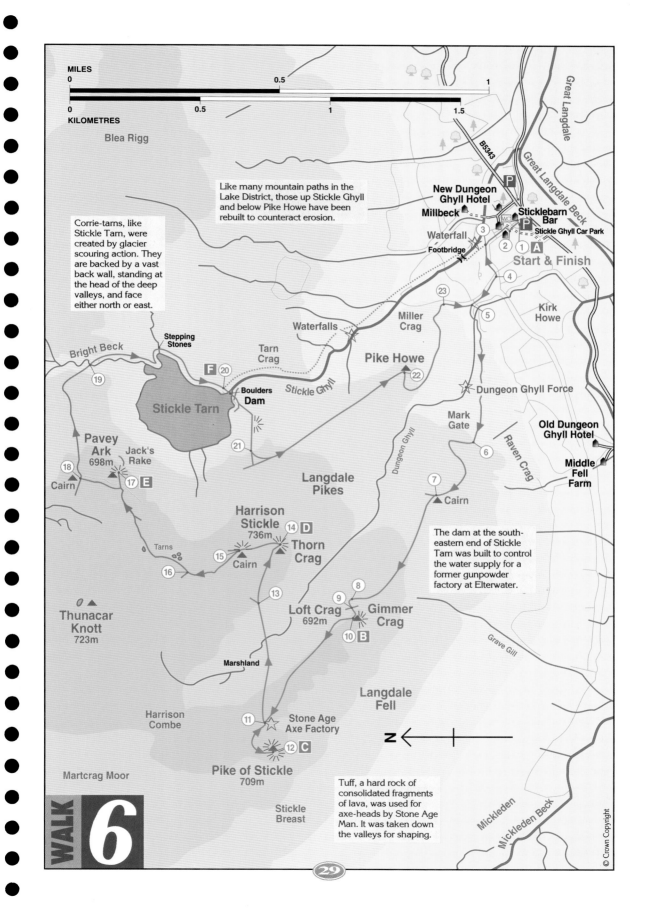

MILES

KILOMETRES

Blea Rigg

Like many mountain paths in the Lake District, those up Stickle Ghyll and below Pike Howe have been rebuilt to counteract erosion.

Corrie-tarns, like Stickle Tarn, were created by glacier scouring action. They are backed by a vast back wall, standing at the head of the deep valleys, and face either north or east.

New Dungeon Ghyll Hotel
Millbeck

Sticklebarn Bar

Waterfall
Footbridge

Stickle Ghyll Car Park
Start & Finish

Kirk Howe

Waterfalls

Miller Crag

Bright Beck

Stepping Stones

Tarn Crag

Pike Howe

Dungeon Ghyll Force

Stickle Ghyll

Boulders
Dam

Stickle Tarn

Mark Gate

Old Dungeon Ghyll Hotel

Raven Crag

Pavey Ark
698m

Jack's Rake

Langdale Pikes

Cairn

Middle Fell Farm

Harrison Stickle
736m

Thorn Crag

Tarns

Cairn

The dam at the south-eastern end of Stickle Tarn was built to control the water supply for a former gunpowder factory at Elterwater.

Thunacar Knott
723m

Loft Crag
692m

Gimmer Crag

Grave Gill

Marshland

Langdale Fell

Harrison Combe

Stone Age Axe Factory

Martcrag Moor

Pike of Stickle
709m

Tuff, a hard rock of consolidated fragments of lava, was used for axe-heads by Stone Age Man. It was taken down the valleys for shaping.

Stickle Breast

Mickleden

Mickleden Beck

WALK **6**

© Crown Copyright

29

WALK 7

OXENDALE-RED TARN-CRINKLE CRAGS-THREE TARNS-HELL GILL
7.6 miles (12.3km)

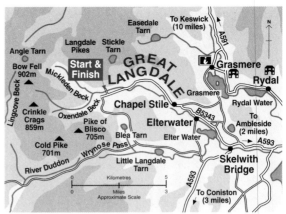

Route Details

Distance	7.6 miles (12.3km)
Degree of Difficulty	Strenuous
Ascent	794m (2,605ft)
Time	6.5 hours

Start and Finish Points

Car park (GR 286061) at the Old Dungeon Ghyll Hotel at the head of Great Langdale.

Follow the A593, from Ambleside, towards Coniston. On approaching Skelwith Bridge, bear right on the B5343. Continue up Great Langdale. Pass the New Dungeon Ghyll Hotel on the right. Continue for 1 mile turning right to the Old Dungeon Ghyll Hotel, near the end of the road.

Maps Needed

OS Outdoor leisure No 6 (1:25 000)
OS Landranger No 90 (1:50 000)
OS Landranger No 89 (1:50 000)

Parking Facilities

The National Trust car park (GR 286061) has services adjacent to it.

Short Cuts

At (14), to avoid The Bad Step ahead, bear left. Follow a narrow cairned rocky path, bending right close to rock walls on the right. Ascend a rake and over rocks onto a col. Bear round right to the summit of the Second Crinkle at (15).

At (20) turn left onto The Band and continue down the clear path as far as (5). Turn left and follow the outward route. (This is shorter in time but less attractive than the Hell Gill route.)

Route Summary

An adventurous walk, crammed with thrills and surprises, its beauty lying in its wildness and craggy desolation. A steady climb out of the Oxendale valley, past the reeded Red Tarn, leads up onto the first of the five Crinkle Crags. From here some scrambling is required to surmount The Bad Step onto the second Crinkle, though it is possible to avoid this minor feat of mountaineering by following a slight detour. The undulating ridge path linking these five pinnacles weaves a sinuous course over and between craggy tors, skirting miniscule tarns. Time should be taken to explore all nooks and crannies of this fascinating ridge whose eastern face is scored with shattered crags and wild scree gullies which plummet into the Oxendale valley below. The descent is equally inspiring, tracing the rim of the deep chasm of Hell Gill, whose thundering waters cascade over the rocky shelves of Whorneyside Force. Below this, the scenery is breathtaking as three gills meet amidst a confusion of rockfalls.

A calm beginning in Great Langdale to the exhilarations ahead

This ridge walk should not be attempted in mist which can make the path confusing and obliterate the magnificent aerial views and rock scenery.

Interesting Features

LANDFORMS Looking west from Great Langdale is a horseshoe range of mountains, stretching from the Langdale Pikes, over Bow Fell, Crinkle Crags and terminating in Pike of Blisco which drops down to Wrynose Bottom. As the eye travels round this arc it is inevitably drawn to the distinctive shape of Crinkle Crags, so-named because of their physical characteristics. Viewed more closely from the head of Great Langdale they are etched into the skyline like the knuckles of a clenched fist. The high serrated edge of five rocky pinnacles and undulations have steep buttresses intersected by precipitous gullies, all plunging (E) down into the Oxendale valley beneath. The western flank is equally significant for its wild rugged desolation, shattered crags dropping sharply down over rocky slopes into the Eskdale valley. If viewed from the Eskdale valley, Crinkle Crags can be seen to be part of another mountain arc which sweeps round from Scafell (N) over Great End, Esk Pike, Bow Fell, Crinkle Crags and Pike of Blisco, Crinkle Crags is flanked (N) by a col on which sits the miniscule Three Tarns below Bow Fell, whilst (SE) is another col containing the reeded Red Tarn below Pike of Blisco.

HISTORY Some of the Lakeland fells, such as Blencathra and Helvellyn, inherited their names from Norse invaders. Others are named after local village settlements such as The Old Man of Coniston, whereas others are called Langdale Pikes or Esk Pike after the valleys from which they rise. Some even carry the names of ancient dalesmen, such as Harrison Stickle or Robinson. Crinkle Crags, like Great Gable or Pillar, have earned their names as a result of their characteristic shapes.

There are no stone walls hereabouts, a fact which testifies to the wildness and rugged desolation of Crinkle Crags which kept early man at a safe distance from such craggy prominences.

VIEWPOINTS From various vantage-points on the five summit cairns of Crinkle Crags (NW) is a splendid view of the Scafell range whose massive bulk obscures any distant sight of the western and north-western fells, except for Crag Hill (NNW). In the foreground (N) are eroded slopes leading up to the conical summit of Bow Fell, beyond which to the right is Glaramara, with distant views (NNE) of

Skiddaw and Blencathra. (NE) over Sergeant Man lies the Helvellyn range, with a fine view of Pike of Stickle and Harrison Stickle, two of the Langdale Pikes, in the foreground. (ESE) down shattered rock buttresses and precipitous scree gullies is a comprehensive and dramatic picture of the Oxendale valley below leading into Great Langdale, and in the distance beyond the High Street range and the Kentmere fells. (E) is Loughrigg Fell and Wansfell Pike. (SE) the view is dominated by Pike of Blisco in the foreground with the Coniston fells to the right of it. Of all the views probably the most beautiful is (SW) over the Duddon and Esk valleys, tracing the course of the winding River Esk down to the Irish Sea at Ravenglass. (W), framed between Whin Rigg and Illgill Head, are the cooling towers of the British Nuclear Fuels power-station at Sellafield. There are several lakes and tarns on view: (ESE) Windermere; (SE) Red Tarn, Esthwaite Water and Wise Een Tarn; and (SW) Devoke Water.

The start and finish point in Great Langdale

A particularly attractive area on the walk lies just below Whorneyside Force where the cascading waters of Hell Gill, Crinkle Gill, and Browney Gill all converge in a tumble of white water amidst a tangle of rocky outcrops, gorges and rockfalls. It is a scene of wild, desolate beauty.

Cross-Section of the Route

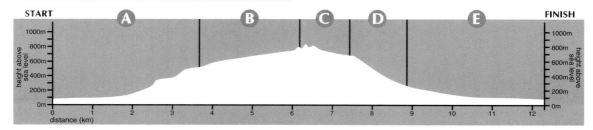

Route Description

SECTION A	2.2 miles (3.5km)	
Destination	Red Tarn (GR 267039)	
Ascent	410m(1345ft)	Descent 0m(0ft)

■ **1** Start from the car park entrance along the entry lane. Turn first left to cross the bridge over Great Langdale Beck. Turn right along the B5343. Go straight across the road at the T-junction.

■ **2** Pass through a gate opposite, at signs to Oxendale/The Band and Stool End Farm. Go ahead along a farm driveway. Pass over a cattle-grid. Ahead, go through a gap between walls. Cross a bridge over Oxendale Beck. Go through a field-gate adjacent to a cattle-grid to the end of the driveway.

■ **3** Bear right through a field-gate at a low-level sign. Enter the yard of Stool End Farm. Turn left round a barn on the left with the farmhouse on the right. Pass through a field-gate to leave the yard.

■ **4** Follow ahead the low-level sign to The Band at a pathway junction. Go up (SW) a broad uphill path along a wall on the left for 100m.

■ **5** Keep ahead, ignoring a right junction which bends up The Band. Go through a gate. Bear right along a wall.

■ **6** Pass through a waymarked kissing-gate to the left of a large sheepfold. Go through a wicket-gate at the end of the sheepfold. Proceed ahead for 75m.

■ **7** Turn left at a pathway junction away from the wall. Cross Oxendale Beck over a footbridge with two memorial plaques. Bear right along the beck on the right for 175m.

■ **8** Bear left (SW) at a large cairn to ascend a reconstructed path. Bend right onto Brown Howe. Continue on a stony path, ascending above the ravine of Browney Gill down on the right. The path bends left, now along Browney Gill on the right.

■ **9** Turn right above the waterfalls on the right. Cross a feeder brook from Red Tarn. Turn left (SSE) uphill along the brook on the left. The path levels out on a col with Red Tarn (530m/1,738ft) ahead.

SECTION B	1.2 miles (2km)	
Destination	Crinkle Crags (GR 251045)	
Ascent	303m(994ft)	Descent 0m(0ft)

■ **10** Turn right (W) at a small cairn on cross-paths. Cross a marshy plateau. The path ascends, bending right, then climbing more steeply as it bends left.

■ **11** Bend right to ford a rivulet at a junction up to Cold Pike. Go ahead to ford another rivulet. The path ascends less steeply, still bending right (NW). Ford a shallow beck at a small tarn on the right. The cairned path bends left (WNW) to ascend a gradual slope to the foot of Crinkle Crags (777m/2,549ft).

SECTION C	1.2 miles (2km)	
Destination	Three Tarns (GR 248060)	
Ascent	81m(266ft)	Descent 162m(531ft)

■ **12** Go up (NW) a short stone-shoot to the rocky summit of the First Crinkle (833m/2,732ft).

■ **13** From the summit keep ahead along the cairned ridge. Bend left down over rocks. Cross a grassy depression with the Second Crinkle ahead.

■ **14** Continue up a steep scree gully blocked by two huge boulders forming The Bad Step. Either climb the short rock-wall to the right using hand-holds, or squeeze through a short narrow tunnel in the rocks on the left. Continue up to the summit of the Second Crinkle (859m/2,817ft). (See Short Cuts for alternative route).

■ **15** From the summit descend ahead to the head of the scree gully of Mickle Door on the right. Proceed ahead, bearing right up to the pyramid summit of the Third Crinkle (835m/2,739ft).

■ **16** From the summit the meandering path descends, bending left then right, just below the summit of the Fourth Crinkle (832m/2,729ft).

■ **17** Continue ahead, bending left then right, just below the summit of the Fifth Crinkle (817m/2,680ft).

■ **18** Go ahead to pass small tarns on the right. Cross over the shoulder of Shelter Crags. Continue ahead to pass a rock-tower on the right. Pass some pools on the left. Descend to cross-paths on the grassy depression of Three Tarns (707m/2,319ft).

SECTION D	1 mile (1.6km)	
Destination	Hell Gill (GR 259054)	
Ascent	0m(0ft)	Descent 382m(1253ft)

■ **19** Turn right (NE) on the path known as The Band. Follow along the infant stream of Buscoe Sike on the right for 30m.

■ **20** Turn right to ford Buscoe Sike. Immediately turn left (E) along the stream on the left, descending steeply the cairned path with a scree slope on the right. The path sweeps right (SE) with the stream down a more gradual grassy slope.

■ **21** Take the right fork in the path at the head of the deep gorge of Hell Gill below on the left. Descend along the edge of the ravine. The path becomes quite steep, descending a short scree slope to a beck.

SECTION E	2 miles (3.2km)	
Destination	Old Dungeon Ghyll Hotel (GR 286061)	
Ascent	0m(0ft)	Descent 250m(820ft)

■ **22** Turn right along the beck on the left for 20m. Turn left to ford the beck. Immediately turn left. Follow the beck round, passing Whorneyside Force. Descend (SE) the side of the ravine on a rocky path with Hell Gill down on the left. The path becomes grassy near the bottom.

■ **23** Turn left over a footbridge with the meeting of the waters below on the right. Immediately turn right. Proceed for 40m.

■ **24** Fork left. Follow a path above Oxendale Beck below on the right for 350m. Bend down right to a wall corner on the left. Proceed along the wall on the left with the beck on the right to (5). Follow the outward route to the car park.

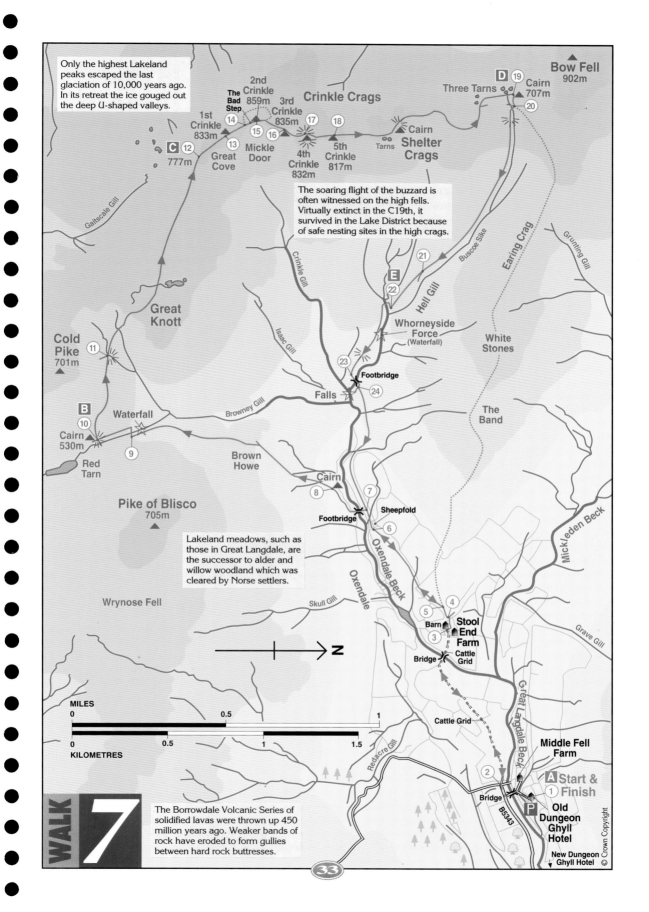

Only the highest Lakeland peaks escaped the last glaciation of 10,000 years ago. In its retreat the ice gouged out the deep U-shaped valleys.

Bow Fell 902m

D 19 Cairn 707m 20

Three Tarns

Crinkle Crags

2nd Crinkle 859m

The Bad Step

1st Crinkle 833m 14

15 16

3rd Crinkle 835m 17 18

C 12 777m

13 Mickle Door

Great Cove

4th Crinkle 832m

5th Crinkle 817m

Tarns

Cairn **Shelter Crags**

The soaring flight of the buzzard is often witnessed on the high fells. Virtually extinct in the C19th, it survived in the Lake District because of safe nesting sites in the high crags.

Gaitscale Gill

Crinkle Gill

Buscoe Sike

Earing Crag

Grunting Gill

21

E 22

Great Knott

Isaac Gill

Whorneyside Force (Waterfall)

Hell Gill

White Stones

Cold Pike 701m 11

23

Footbridge

Falls 24

The Band

B 10 Waterfall

Cairn 530m

9

Browney Gill

Red Tarn

Brown Howe

Pike of Blisco 705m

Cairn 8

7

Footbridge

Sheepfold

6

Lakeland meadows, such as those in Great Langdale, are the successor to alder and willow woodland which was cleared by Norse settlers.

Oxendale Beck

Mickleden Beck

Wrynose Fell

Skull Gill

Oxendale

4

5

Barn

Stool End Farm

3

Grave Gill

Bridge

Cattle Grid

MILES

| 0 | | 0.5 | | 1 |

KILOMETRES

| 0 | | 0.5 | | 1 | | 1.5 |

N

Cattle Grid

Redacre Gill

Middle Fell Farm

2

Great Langdale Beck

A Start & Finish 1

Bridge

B5343

P

Old Dungeon Ghyll Hotel

New Dungeon Ghyll Hotel

WALK 7

The Borrowdale Volcanic Series of solidified lavas were thrown up 450 million years ago. Weaker bands of rock have eroded to form gullies between hard rock buttresses.

WALK 8

BOW FELL-
ESK PIKE-
ANGLE TARN-
ROSSETT PIKE-
STAKE GILL
9.6 miles (15.4km)

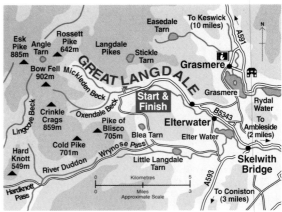

Route Details

Distance	9.6 miles (15.4km)
Degree of Difficulty	Strenuous
Ascent	1,003m (3,289ft)
Time	8.5 hours

Start and Finish Points

Car park (GR 286061) at the Old Dungeon Ghyll Hotel at the head of Great Langdale.

Follow the A593 from Ambleside towards Coniston. On approaching Skelwith Bridge, bear right on the B5343. Continue up Great Langdale. Pass the New Dungeon Ghyll Hotel over to the right. Continue for 1 mile as far as the Old Dungeon Ghyll Hotel on the right near the end of the road.

Maps Needed

OS Outdoor Leisure No 6 (1:25 000)
OS Landranger No 90 (1:50 000)
OS Landranger No 89 (1:50 000)

Parking Facilities

The car park (GR 286061) has services adjacent to it.

Short Cuts

At (6) veer left on The Band. Turn right (N) on the col at Three Tarns. Proceed to (10). Route to be used in bad weather and by less experienced walkers.

At (7) continue steeply up the side of the rock buttress on a direct route to (10).

At (12) fork right (N), descending a rough rocky path. Filter right at the main path junction to (!6).

At (17) continue ahead. Bend left down Rossett Gill on a steep, rocky path to (22).

Route Summary

The imposing pyramid of Bow Fell invites conquest when viewed from a distance. Pastureland of Great Langdale, at its eastern base, marks a subdued start to the expedition. Anticipation mounts with every tread up the rising slopes of The Band. The exciting narrow shelf path of the climbers' traverse should only be attempted in good weather by more experienced walkers. Otherwise follow the Three Tarns route. The final ascent up a rocky stairway leads to the jumbled mass of naked rock which tapers to the pointed summit of Bow Fell. Views from here, as well as Esk Pike further along the ridge, are exceptional, with an excellent profile of the Scafell range close-at-hand and a long prospect down the Esk valley to the Irish Sea.

The Band and flat-topped Rossett Pike overlooking Mickleden

Over the broad plateau of Esk Hause, an easy descent leads to Angle Tarn, couched beneath the crags of Bow Fell. Ahead lies the summit of Rossett Pike, a vantage-point for aerial contemplation of Mickleden valley, the towering Langdale Pikes, and a study of the northern cliffs of Bow Fell. An aerial traverse of the final ridge, a twisting descent of the last stages of Stake Pass path, leaves a quiet return along the floor of the Mickleden valley.

Interesting Features

LANDFORMS Bow Fell, viewed from a distance, presents itself as a very distinctive pyramid on the Lakeland skyscape. This shapely peak is remarkable for its graceful symmetrical form, standing proud at the head of three dales and serving as a watershed to valley streams which flow into three rivers; Great Langdale (E) and the River Brathay; Langstrath (N) and the River Derwent; Eskdale (SW) and the River Esk. Bow Fell stands at the hub of two curving mountain ranges: one stretching round from Scafell to the west, the other from the Langdale Pikes to the east, and both terminating at Wrynose Pass below Pike of Blisco to the south-east. Bow Fell is linked to Crinkle Crags (S) by a col on which sits the miniscule Three Tarns, and to Esk Pike (N) by the pass of Ore Gap. Not only is it classical in its shape, but it typifies so many Lakeland climbs in that it rises from flat valley pastures, giving way to rougher and steeper slopes, and culminating in a summit approach over boulders and naked rock and up scree slopes. The craggy summit pyramid stands on top of a sloping eastern plinth of flat rock, appropriately named Flat Crags, which suddenly plunges into the valley below. Particularly imposing is the northern downfall where the shattered crags of the Bow Fell Buttress drop down over Hanging Knotts to Angle Tarn.

Esk Pike is situated on a ridge midway between Great End (NW) to which it is linked by the broad grassy plateau of Esk Hause, and Bow Fell (SE) over Ore Gap. It lies at the head of upper Eskdale. Its long craggy southern ridge is bounded (W) by the River Esk and (E) by Yeastyrigg Gill. Its northern ridge descends into Langstrath.

VIEWPOINTS As befitting a perfect pyramid, the summit of Bow Fell is a magnificent viewpoint, its steep sloping sides creating no obstructions and lending depth as well as distance to surrounding valleys and fells. (N) on the skyline is Skiddaw and Blencathra, whilst (NE) is the Helvellyn range, with St Sunday Crag and Fairfield beyond Sergeant Man. Moving (E) over the near pinnacles of the Langdale Pikes, the High Street range and the Kentmere Fells dominate the horizon. (ESE) across Great Langdale, over Loughrigg Fell, part of Windermere can be discerned backed by the distant Pennines. (SE), just to the left of the summit of Pike of Blisco, is a glimpse of distant Esthwaite Water, whilst to its right Red Tarn fronts the rounded bulk of Wetherlam. (SSE) over Three Tarns and Crinkle Crags lie the summits of the Old Man of Coniston and Dow Crag. (SSW) the eye travels over Mosedale and the Duddon valley to Hard Knott and over Harter Fell to the distant hump of Black Combe, rising from the unseen Irish Sea. (SW) there is a marvellous view down Eskdale tracing the River Esk to its estuary, with Devoke Water perched on the fell above. The spectacular skyline (W) to (N) contains, amongst a string of mountains, Scafell, Scafell Pike, Pillar, Great End, Great Gable, Green Gable, Grasmoor, Robinson, Crag Hill, Grisedale Pike and Dale Head.

Bow Fell towering above the plains of Great Langdale

Many of the views from Esk Pike are similar to those from Bow Fell. However there is a nearer, enhanced aspect of the Scafells (W), and Derwent Water (NNE) is brought into the picture. (S) opens up the view of the Duddon estuary, and 40m north of the summit Angle Tarn can be seen (E) below.

Rossett Pike, inferior in height to Bow Fell and Esk Pike, may not have the same distant views, but excels as a vantage-point for a close-up of the Langdale Pikes (E) and aerial contemplation down the deep Mickleden valley below. There is also an opportunity to study the tangled rock structure of the northern cliffs of Bow Fell.

Cross-Section of the Route

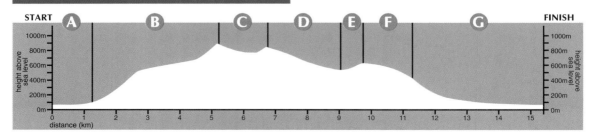

Route Description

SECTION A	0.8 miles (1.3km)	
Destination	The Band (GR 276057)	
Ascent	15m(49ft)	**Descent** 0m(0ft)

■ **1** Start from the car park entrance along the entry lane (WSW). Turn first left to cross the bridge over Great Langdale Beck. Turn right along the B5343. Go straight across the road at the T-junction.

■ **2** Pass through a kissing-gate opposite, at signs to Oxendale/The Band and Stool End Farm. Go ahead (WSW) along a farm driveway. Pass through a field-gate adjacent to a cattle-grid. Ahead, go through a gap between walls. Cross a bridge over Oxendale Beck. Go through a field-gate adjacent to a cattle-grid to the end of the driveway.

■ **3** Bear right through a field-gate at a low-level sign. Enter the yard of Stool End Farm. Turn left round a barn on the left with the farmhouse on the right. Pass through a field-gate to leave the farmyard.

■ **4** Follow ahead the low-level sign to The Band at a pathway junction. Go up a broad uphill path along a wall on the left for 100m.

SECTION B	2.2 miles (3.6km)	
Destination	Bow Fell (GR 245064)	
Ascent	792m(2598ft)	**Descent** 0m(0ft)

■ **5** Turn right (W) at the top of the rise. Follow a stony uphill path, known as The Band. Pass through a kissing-gate adjacent to a high ladder-stile at a commemorative seat. Continue to climb The Band (WNW) on a winding path for 1.4 miles.

■ **6** Fork right, off The Band, at three adjacent cairns on a broad grassy plateau. (Less experienced walkers, and in bad weather, proceed ahead (W) via the Three Tarns route). Ascend (NW) a narrow stony path as far as a rock buttress up ahead.

■ **7** Fork right down a narrow path, known as Climbers' Traverse. Follow along a narrow undulating ledge with a rock wall to the left and a steep drop on the right. Continue for 400m.

■ **8** Fork left, uphill, round a rock buttress of Flat Crags. Proceed for 100m to a waterspout emerging from the base of Cambridge Crag.

■ **9** Double back left at a cairn. Ascend a steep twisting rocky path (SSW) between a rock wall on the right and a band of boulders on the left.

■ **10** Bear right at the top of the ascent. Follow a cairned path which bends right over boulders to the summit cairn of Bow Fell (902m/2,959ft).

SECTION C	1 mile (1.6km)	
Destination	Esk Pike (GR 237075)	
Ascent	104m(340ft)	**Descent** 121m(397ft)

■ **11** Leave (N) the summit down a cairned boulder-field to a plateau. The broad stony path bends left (NNW), gradually descending and swinging further left (W) over another boulder-field.

■ **12** Cross the col of Ore Gap. Ascend (NW) over a series of stony shelves to the summit cairn of Esk Pike (885m/2,903ft).

SECTION D	1.7 miles (2.7km)	
Destination	Angle Tarn (GR 245078)	
Ascent	0m(0ft)	**Descent** 335m(1099ft)

■ **13** Leave the cairn (NW) down a narrow boulder-field. The path levels out, bending right over a flat slab of rock. Continue to descend gradually to cross-paths on the broad grassy depression of Esk Hause.

■ **14** Turn right at a cairn. Follow a broad downhill path (NE) to a stone shelter on the right.

■ **15** Turn right (ESE) onto a descending bridleway path. Ford Allencrags Gill. Continue ahead slightly uphill, passing between small tarns on the plateau of Tongue Head. Go downhill to Angle Tarn.

SECTION E	0.4 miles (0.6km)	
Destination	Rossett Pike (GR 249075)	
Ascent	92m(302ft)	**Descent** 0m(0ft)

■ **16** Ford Angletarn Gill. Bear left on the bridleway, bending right (SE) as it climbs. Keep ahead, ignoring a left branch.

■ **17** Turn left (E) at the top of the rise, 40m before a cairn ahead. Follow a narrow grassy path, winding up to the summit cairn of Rossett Pike (642m/2,106ft).

SECTION F	1 mile (1.6km)	
Destination	Stake Gill (GR 260082)	
Ascent	0m(0ft)	**Descent** 272m(892ft)

■ **18** Leave the cairn (ENE) along the escarpment on the right. Follow a narrow faint path to a second cairn ahead.

■ **19** Turn left, bending right on a thin winding grassy path between rocks. Gradually descend to a depression. Follow a faint path (NE) through a grassy channel between rocky mounds. Go downhill with the cairn of Buck Pike up on the right. Bend right over Littlegill Head.

■ **20** Filter right onto a thin descending path over Black Crags. Bend right (E) to arrive at Stake Gill on the Stake Pass path.

SECTION G	2.5 miles (4km)	
Destination	Old Dungeon Ghyll Hotel (GR 286061)	
Ascent	0m(0ft)	**Descent** 275m(902ft)

■ **21** Turn right (S) on the broad Stake Pass bridleway, parallel to Stake Gill on the left. Follow down a zig-zagging path.

■ **22** Turn left at the bottom at a sheepfold on the right at a pathway junction. Cross a footbridge over Mickleden Beck. Turn right (SE). Follow the bridleway for 1.7 miles along Mickleden Beck on the right. Go through a field-gate passing behind the hotel and down into the car park.

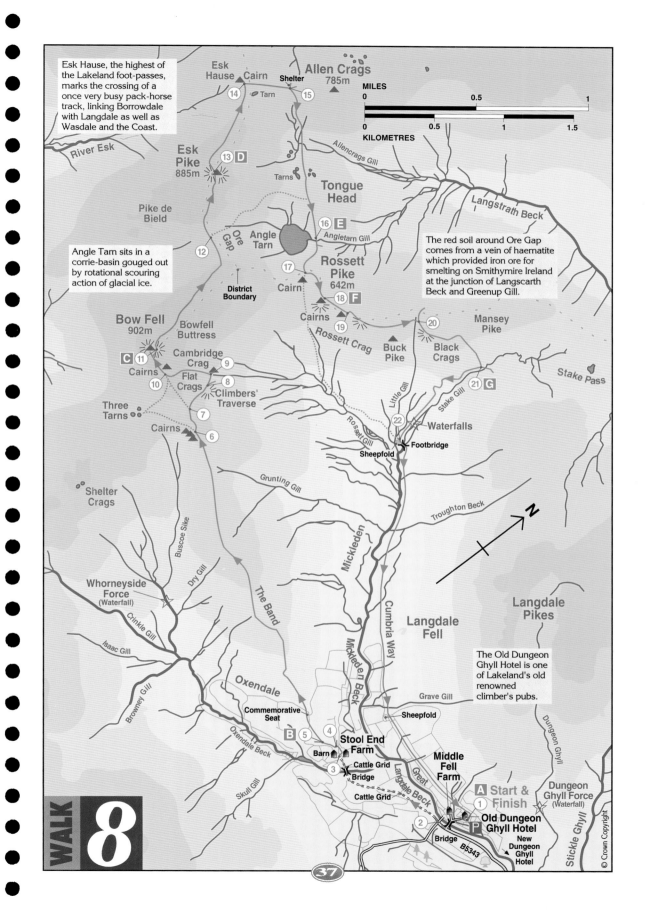

Esk Hause, the highest of the Lakeland foot-passes, marks the crossing of a once very busy pack-horse track, linking Borrowdale with Langdale as well as Wasdale and the Coast.

Angle Tarn sits in a corrie-basin gouged out by rotational scouring action of glacial ice.

The red soil around Ore Gap comes from a vein of haematite which provided iron ore for smelting on Smithymire Ireland at the junction of Langscarth Beck and Greenup Gill.

The Old Dungeon Ghyll Hotel is one of Lakeland's old renowned climber's pubs.

MILES
0   0.5   1

KILOMETRES
0   0.5   1   1.5

Allen Crags 785m
Esk Hause Cairn
Shelter
Tarn
14 15

Esk Pike 885m
13 D
Tongue Head
Tarns
River Esk
Allencrags Gill
Langstrath Beck

Pike de Bield
Ore Gap
Angle Tarn
12
16 E
Angletarn Gill

District Boundary
17
Cairn
Rossett Pike 642m
18 F

Bow Fell 902m
Bowfell Buttress
Cairns
C 11
10
Cambridge Crag 9
Flat Crags 8
Climbers' Traverse
7
Cairns 19
Rossett Crag
Buck Pike
Black Crags
Mansey Pike
20
Stake Pass
21 G
Little Gill
Stake Gill

Three Tarns
Cairns 6

Shelter Crags
Rossett Gill
22
Waterfalls
Sheepfold
Footbridge

Grunting Gill
Buscoe Sike
Dry Gill

Troughton Beck
N

Whorneyside Force (Waterfall)
Crinkle Gill
Isaac Gill
The Band
Mickleden
Cumbria Way
Langdale Fell
Langdale Pikes

Browney Gill
Oxendale
Commemorative Seat
B 5
Barn
3
4
Stool End Farm
Cattle Grid
Bridge
Cattle Grid
Oxendale Beck
Skull Gill

Mickleden Beck
Great Langdale Beck
Grave Gill
Sheepfold
Middle Fell Farm
Dungeon Ghyll

A Start & Finish
1
2
Bridge
B5343
Old Dungeon Ghyll Hotel
New Dungeon Ghyll Hotel
Dungeon Ghyll Force (Waterfall)
Stickle Ghyll

© Crown Copyright

WALK 8

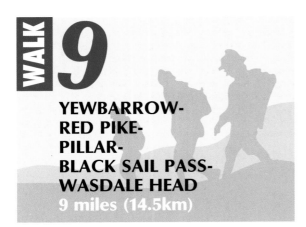

WALK 9

YEWBARROW-RED PIKE-PILLAR-BLACK SAIL PASS-WASDALE HEAD
9 miles (14.5km)

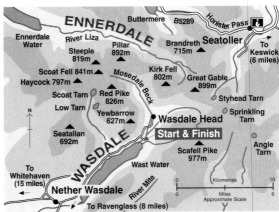

Route Details

Distance	9 miles (14.5km)
Degree of Difficulty	Strenuous
Ascent	1,095m (3,591ft)
Time	8 hours

Start and Finish Points

Car park (GR 182075) on the edge of a campsite at the head of Wast Water.

Leave the A595 at Gosforth. Travel east through Nether Wasdale. Follow the road along the north-western shore of Wast Water. At the head of the lake, turn right at the sign to the campsite, or park in limited lay-by parking opposite the entrance road.

Maps Needed

OS Outdoor Leisure No 6 (1:25 000)
OS Outdoor Leisure No 4 (1:25 000)
OS Landranger No 89 (1:50 000)

Parking Facilities

There is also a car park (GR 187085) 1 mile north along the road near Wasdale Head Inn.

Short Cuts

At (6) continue ahead (NNW). Gradually ascend the valley to (8).

At (8) is a very steep descent (N) of Dorehead Screes. Bend right (SE) at the bottom to (18).

At (12) at Wind Gap, turn right (SE) down a long, steep, stony slope to just after (17).

At (13) descend (N) on the alternative, but longer, high level route which emerges above (14). (Only for more experienced walkers in good weather.)

Route Summary

Mosedale branches north-west from Wasdale Head. The circuit of its ridges is known as The Mosedale Horseshoe, one of Lakeland's most exhilarating ridge walks. The route can be as long or short as time and energy dictates, giving multiple choices. The first choice is either scrambling at both ends of the rocky spine of Yewbarrow with panoramic views, or a gradual ascent along the western slopes of Yewbarrow to Dore Head col. A steady climb leads to a rocky outcrop in the form of a chair, only a short stride from the subsidiary summit of Red Pike, and on to its principal cairn, poised on an escarpment of jagged crags, plummeting into Mosedale.

Pillar seen above Mosedale from Wasdale Head packhorse bridge

An escarpment traverse gives an optional diversion, from the ridge path, going over Scoat Fell to Steeple and rejoining the ridge path over Wind Gap onto Pillar. Again there is a choice of an easy descent with superb aerial views along the eastern ridge, or, in good weather only, to follow the high level route via the Shamrock Traverse amidst magnificent mountain scenery with close-up views of Pillar Rock. Both routes lead to Black Sail Pass and a leisurely descent into lower Mosedale and Wasdale.

Interesting Features

LANDFORMS Yewbarrow is an elongated mountain with a high narrow ridge which stretches for two miles, its eastern flank descending into Wasdale, and at the northern end down into Mosedale. Its western slopes drop down to Over Beck which rises at Dore Head, the col linking Yewbarrow to Red Pike. Red Pike is a mountain of contrasts, its mile-long eastern face of splintered crags dramatically plunges 610 metres (2,000ft) into Mosedale, whilst its western slope declines more gradually to Nether Beck, encountering Scoat Tarn and Low Tarn on the way. (N) lies Scoat Fell, with Steeple ahead.

Steeple, Pillar, Kirk Fell and Great Gable are the magnificent peaks which dominate the head of the afforested Ennerdale valley, along which the River Liza winds for five miles before entering Ennerdale Water. Pillar, despite the steepness of its southern downfall into Mosedale and the tangled mass of shattered rocks and scree which cascade down its northern face into Ennerdale, has a surprisingly smooth and rounded summit, supporting a triangulation column and two shelters. Its western ridge drops steeply into Wind Gap, whilst its long eastern ridge descends to Black Sail Pass, separating the deep U-shaped glacial bowl of Mosedale from the desolate wastes of upper Ennerdale and the lower western slopes of Kirk Fell.

VIEWPOINTS The whole circuit is one continuous viewpoint, a panorama of distant peaks as well as close-ups of dramatic rock structures, with shattered cliff faces, awe-inspiring buttresses, splintered fissures, and tumbling scree slopes all competing for attention. An early sign of exciting things to come is the approach to the Yewbarrow ridge where through a cleft in the rocks, called Great Door, there is a fine view of Scafell (SE). The grassy summit is a relaxing place from which to study the nearby towering Wasdale Fells with Pillar (N), Kirk Fell and Great Gable (NE), Great End (E). Moving right, are Lingmell, Broad Crag, Scafell Pike and Scafell. (NNW) is Red Pike. In the far distance (NNE), between Hindscarth and Robinson in the middle-ground, Skiddaw can be discerned, as can Helvellyn (ENE), which with Scafell and Scafell Pike gives Yewbarrow summit the distinction of bringing all Lakeland's 900 metres (3,000ft) mountains into view at once. Water on view is Low Tarn (NW), Burnmoor Tarn (SSE) and Wast Water (SW).

Before leaving the subsidiary summit of Red Pike, Scoat Tarn can be seen below (SW). At the principal summit cairn, teetering on the escarpment edge, it is the full length prospect (NNE) from the top of Pillar down over Black Comb at the head of the Mosedale valley which commands attention. In the foreground (ESE) Kirk Fell and Great Gable dominate the scene and the Scafell range (SE) is seen at its best, with the Coniston fells in the distance to the right. Close-at-hand Yewbarrow sits between Harter Fell and Green Crag in the middle distance. (E) lies the Helvellyn range with High Street on the horizon beyond.

The slopes of Yewbarrow dropping steeply into Wast Water

After bending right over Little Scoat Fell where the ridge narrows, the rugged prospect on both sides is superb. (SE) is another view down the Mosedale valley, but the view (WNW) of the eastern downfall of Steeple dropping into Wind Gap Cove and down into Ennerdale is breathtaking.

By the time the summit of Pillar is reached the near and distant fells will have become familiar. There is a grandstand all-round view of most of the Lakeland peaks, except the Coniston fells. Even the Isle of Man can be seen (WSW) on a good day. But, again it is the downward view (N) which holds pride of place. 122 metres (400ft) below is the top of Pillar Rock, an awe-inspiring buttress rising sheer for 150 metres (500ft) from the scree slopes of Ennerdale.

Cross-Section of the Route

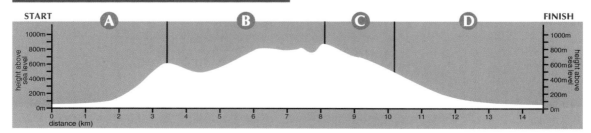

Route Description

SECTION A	1.8 miles (2.9km)		
Destination	Yewbarrow (GR 174085)		
Ascent	547m(1794ft)	Descent	0m(0ft)

■ **1** Start from the car park along the entry lane (NW) over the bridge across Lingmell Beck.

■ **2** Turn left along the road. Proceed for 0.7 miles.

■ **3** Filter right, off the road where it bends down left, 400m before Overbeck Bridge. Follow a footpath sign along a level grassy bankside path. Cross over a stile adjacent to a field-gate in a wire fence.

■ **4** Turn right (N) at cross-paths. Go up to a wall. Turn right (NNE), uphill, keeping the wall close on the left.

■ **5** Turn left over a ladder-stile. Follow a gradually ascending path for 150m.

■ **6** Fork right. Ascend (NNE) towards Dropping Crag, bending right up a steep path to the right of it. Keep ahead with some scrambling over rocks to the left of a broad stony gully. Bear right at the top of the gully. Go up a slope onto the ridge to the left of Great Door. Bend left (NNE). Ascend to the summit cairn and triangulation pillar of Yewbarrow (628m/2,060ft).

SECTION B	1.9 miles (3km)		
Destination	Red Pike (GR 165107)		
Ascent	412m(1350ft)	Descent	214m(702ft)

■ **7** Leave the summit cairn (NNE), descending the north ridge. Cross a depression. Ascend to the cairn on the top of Stirrup Crag (616m/2,020ft). Bear left and descend (NW), initially scrambling steeply down over rocks.

■ **8** Go straight over cross-paths at the col at Dore Head. Ascend a cairned twisting path (WNW) up the southern slope of Red Pike. Pass over a series of grassy shelves. Climb over the rocks to The Chair to the left of the path. Proceed to a subsidiary summit cairn (802m/2,629ft).

■ **9** Bear right (NNE) up a gradual slope to the escarpment edge and the summit cairn of Red Pike (826m/2,709ft).

SECTION C	1.3 miles (2.1km)		
Destination	Pillar (GR 171121)		
Ascent	136m(447ft)	Descent	70m(229ft)

■ **10** Keep ahead along the escarpment edge.

■ **11** If the choice is to ascend Steeple, take the left fork (NW). Climb up the slopes of Great Scoat Fell, bending right (NNW) to the summit of Steeple (819m/2,686ft). Turn round and follow the escarpment edge (E) to join the route.

If not, take a right fork. Follow an ascending path, bending right (NNE) up Little Scoat Fell. The ridge narrows. Continue ahead up to the cairn on the western summit of Wind Gap. Descend, initially scrambling down rocks, to the narrow col

of Wind Gap.

■ **12** Go ahead (NE), scrambling over rocks in the early stages up the western face of Wind Gap. The cairned path leads up the broad rounded summit and the shelters and triangulation pillar at the top of Pillar (892m/2,926ft).

SECTION D	1.5 miles (2.4km)		
Destination	Black Sail Pass (GR 192114)		
Ascent	0m(0ft)	Descent	343m(1125ft)

■ **13** If the choice is to follow the high level route (for more experienced walkers and only in good weather), descend steeply (N) to above Pillar Rock at Pisgah. Bend right (SSE) round the rescue box on the right. The path bends left, then right down the Shamrock Traverse. At the end of the Traverse bend left (NE) down a scree slope with a low rock shelf on the left. The path bends right (SSE), across boulders to pass Robinson's Cairn. Continue ahead (SE) to emerge on the eastern ridge path above (14).

If the choice is the easier route, leave the summit (SE) on the eastern ridge path. Follow some iron fence-posts (ESE) round the escarpment ridge with Ennerdale far below on the left. After descending rocks, bear right (SE), away from the fence-posts. Follow a path down a gradual grassy slope, before picking up the fence-posts and escarpment edge again on the left.

■ **14** Bear right, at the foot of rocks, again temporarily leaving the fence-posts. Follow a grassy path, by-passing Looking Stead (627m/2,057ft) up on the left. Rejoin the fence-posts at a small tarn on the left. Drop down gradually (SE) to cross-paths on the col of Black Sail Pass.

SECTION E	2.5 miles (4.1km)		
Destination	Car Park (GR 182075)		
Ascent	0m(0ft)	Descent	468m(1535ft)

■ **15** Turn right, passing a large cairn on the right. The rocky downhill path bends right (N), then left (SW).

■ **16** Turn left, after descending a zig-zag path. Ford Gatherstone Beck above the falls. Turn right and bend left (S) down the path with a parallel wall up on the left.

■ **17** Go over a stile adjacent to a wicket-gate. The path flattens out, bending left (SSE). After a short rise, pass over another stile adjacent to a wicket-gate. The downhill path (S) follows a wall on the right. Pass through a field-gate with a wall on the left and Mosedale Beck on the right.

■ **18** Turn right over a small humpback packhorse bridge just before the Wasdale Head Inn ahead. Immediately turn left along Mosedale Beck on the left and a wall on the right. Keep along the beck to pass through a field-gate and continue ahead along the clear path.

■ **19** Pass through a kissing-gate with Down in the Dale Bridge on the left. Go ahead (SSW) along the road for 700m. Turn left at (2) into the car park.

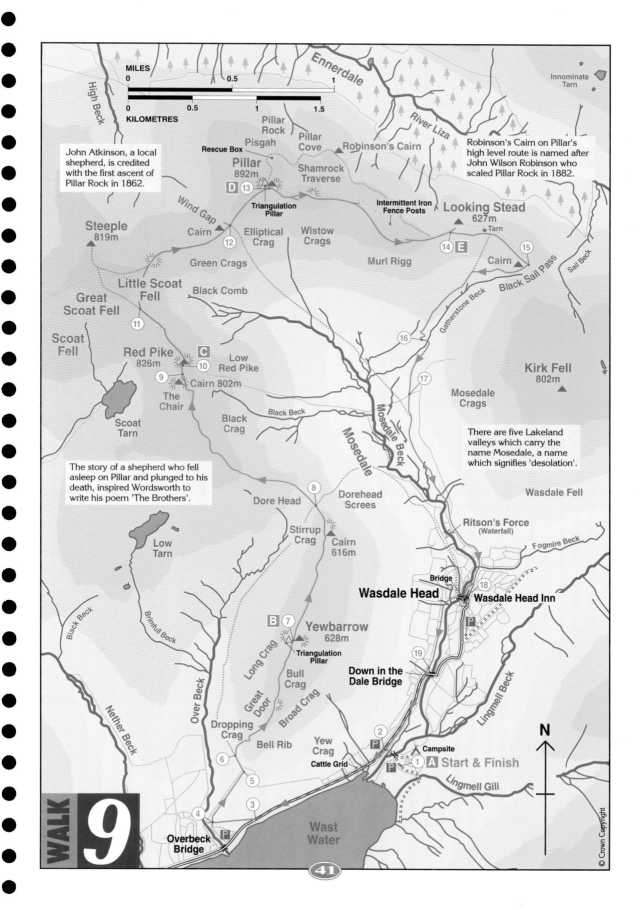

MILES
0   0.5   1

KILOMETRES
0   0.5   1   1.5

Ennerdale

Innominate Tarn

River Liza

High Beck

Pillar Rock
Pisgah
Pillar Cove
Robinson's Cairn

Rescue Box

John Atkinson, a local shepherd, is credited with the first ascent of Pillar Rock in 1862.

Pillar
892m

Shamrock Traverse

D 13

Robinson's Cairn on Pillar's high level route is named after John Wilson Robinson who scaled Pillar Rock in 1882.

Triangulation Pillar

Intermittent Iron Fence Posts

Looking Stead
627m

Wind Gap

Cairn 12

Elliptical Crag

Wistow Crags

Tarn

Steeple
819m

Green Crags

Murl Rigg

14 E

15

Cairn

Black Comb

Black Sail Pass

Sail Beck

Little Scoat Fell

Gatherstone Beck

Great Scoat Fell

11

16

Scoat Fell

Red Pike
826m

C

Low Red Pike

Kirk Fell
802m

9

10

Cairn 802m

17

The Chair

Cairn 802m

Mosedale Crags

Scoat Tarn

Black Crag

Black Beck

Mosedale Beck

There are five Lakeland valleys which carry the name Mosedale, a name which signifies 'desolation'.

The story of a shepherd who fell asleep on Pillar and plunged to his death, inspired Wordsworth to write his poem 'The Brothers'.

Mosedale

Wasdale Fell

Dore Head

8

Dorehead Screes

Ritson's Force
(Waterfall)

Fogmire Beck

Low Tarn

Stirrup Crag

Cairn
616m

Brimfull Beck

Bridge

Wasdale Head

18

Wasdale Head Inn

Black Beck

Long Crag

B 7

Yewbarrow
628m

P

Over Beck

Triangulation Pillar

19

Great Door

Bull Crag

Down in the Dale Bridge

Lingmell Beck

Nether Beck

Dropping Crag

Broad Crag

N

Bell Rib

Yew Crag

2

P

Campsite

6

Cattle Grid

P

1 A Start & Finish

5

Lingmell Gill

4

3

P

Wast Water

Overbeck Bridge

© Crown Copyright

© Copyright

WALK 9

10

HOOKER CRAG-MUNCASTER FELL-MITERDALE-BURNMOOR TARN-RAVENGLASS RAILWAY

12.8 miles (20.5km)

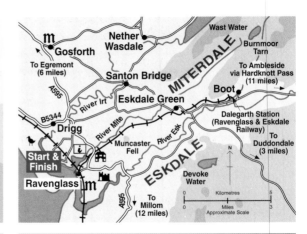

Route Details

Distance	12.8 miles (20.5km)
Degree of Difficulty	Moderate/Strenuous
Ascent	531m (1,742ft)
Time	8.5 hours

Start and Finish Points

Ravenglass car park (GR 085964).

From Windermere, take the A592 to Newby Bridge. Turn right on the A590. At Greenodd, turn right on the A5092. At Grizebeck go ahead on the A595, through Broughton-in-Furness to Whicham. Turn right to follow the A595 (N) to Ravenglass.

From Cockermouth, take the A5086 (S) to Egremont. Turn left onto the A595 and proceed to Ravenglass.

Maps Needed

OS Outdoor Leisure No 6 (1:25 000)
OS Landranger No 89 (1:50 000)
OS Landranger No 96 (1:50 000)

Parking Facilities

The car park is behind the Ratty Arms behind the Ravenglass Railway Station. Toilets. Tourist Information Centre and Museum at Ravenglass Railway Station and services in the village.

Short Cuts

At (9) proceed ahead to (11), so omitting the summit of Hooker Crag.

At (15) turn right into Irton Road Railway Station. Take the Ratty train on the Ravenglass and Eskdale Railway back to (1) at Ravenglass, so omitting Miterdale.

Route Summary

This linear walk combines scenic variety with historical attractions: the ancient port of Ravenglass; a Roman bath-house; a lane thought to be the site of a section of a Roman road; Muncaster Castle which Ruskin described as 'the gateway to paradise'; and finally a delightful ride through the splendours of Eskdale on a miniature railway with a chequered industrial past. Leaving the coast, paths meander through mixed woodland and rhododendron groves. The traverse of Muncaster Fell, past tiny tree-fringed Muncaster Tarn and over Hooker Crag, reveal a charming panorama, seawards across to the Isle of Man and inland over lower Eskdale to Lakeland's highest mountains.

Historic Eskdale Mill at the foot of the corpse road into Boot

The climb up picturesque Miterdale along the tinkling River Mite gradually enters wilder country. Then to Burnmoor Tarn, over the rim of a craggy combe which inspired Arthur Ransome's 'Swallows and the Amazons'. From the tarn, the route descends moorland on an Old Corpse path into Eskdale, past historic Eskdale Mill in the attractive village of Boot. The return to Ravenglass by rail brings a restful and scenic end to a stimulating walk.

Interesting Features

LANDFORMS Rising gradually from the coast is the ridge of Muncaster Fell which divides the broad farmland of Miterdale (N) and the Eskdale valley (S). On the fringe of the Borrowdale Volcanic mountain structure, the topography is characterised by rolling fell with some igneous intrusions.

Once over Muncaster Fell and ascending Miterdale, the surrounding landscape becomes more craggy as the route begins a steady penetration into Borrowdale Volcanic territory.

Eskdale stretches from the foot of the Scafells to the coast at Ravenglass. Its middle reaches mark the division between the Borrowdale Volcanic Series and the Eskdale granite, so creating glorious scenery, though Eskdale has no lake.

HISTORY Ravenglass was a Saxon port. The Roman general, Agricola, built a guardian fort (Glannoventa) from which maybe an unfulfilled invasion of Ireland was intended. From this supply-base, the Romans reconstructed the Anglo-Saxon road (E) over Muncaster Fell to their fort on Hardknott Pass, and onwards to another fort at Ambleside (Galava). From here, the final stretch of the highest Roman road in Britain, High Street, leads (E) over the fells to Brougham (Brocavum) near Penrith. The Roman fort at Ravenglass was destroyed in the late C19th to make way for the Cumbrian coastal railway.

At the confluence of the rivers Irt, Mite and Esk, where they flow into the sea, Ravenglass lost its importance as a port when the harbour silted up. Compensation lies in the fact that it is now a quiet seaside hamlet with expansive dunes and saltings, serving as Nature Reserves.

Like most Cumbrian castles, Muncaster Castle was originally fortified with a 'pele' tower, built in 1325 by the Pennington family as protection against marauding Scots. In the 1860s it was converted into a mansion, and today it remains the Pennington ancestral home which is open to the public during the summer months. The grounds, set against a backdrop of the high fells, are at their best when azaleas and rhododendrons are in bloom.

Eskdale has a long history: Neolithic man carved his stone axes from the rock at its head, bringing them down to be sharpened on the coastal sandstone; the Romans reconstructed the Anglo-Saxon road; the Vikings settled here; after the Norman conquest, deer herds were managed by the monks of Furness Abbey; from Roman times until 1882 high quality iron ore (haematite) was extracted from the dale's pink granite.

A narrow-gauge railway was opened in 1872 to carry iron ore from the mines at Boot down to the main line at Ravenglass. The cost of its construction, £42,000, pushed up the price of the ore, so the railway closed in 1882. In 1876 a passenger service was introduced, closed down in 1913, and was put back into service in 1915. In 1949 it was bought by the Keswick Granite Company when the quarries re-opened at Beckfoot. In 1960 it was bought for £12,000 by the Ravenglass and Eskdale Preservation Society. Today 'La'al Ratty', as the little train is affectionately known, is a tourist attraction as well as providing a commuter link between the Eskdale valley and the main line at Ravenglass.

Quiet Ravenglass, once a busy Roman port and fort

VIEWPOINTS Though Muncaster Fell is only moderate in height, its traverse offers excellent views of lower Eskdale, and the eminence of Hooker Crag gives a panoramic prospect seawards (W), and (NE) to the Scafells, Crinkle Crag and Bow Fell.

From Burnmoor Tarn there are splendid upward views (NE) of the western facade of Scafell Pike and the crags of Illgill Head (WNW).

Cross-Section of the Route

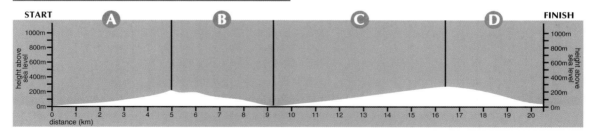

Route Description

SECTION A	3.3 miles (5.3km)	
Destination	Hooker Crag (GR 112983)	
Ascent	231m(758ft)	Descent 0m(0ft)

■ **1** Start by leaving the car park from the opposite corner (SE) to the entrance. Cross a railway footbridge. Fork right along a short path.

■ **2** Turn right (S) on a narrow road at a sign to Newtown Knott/Muncaster. Pass Walls Castle on the left. Proceed for 150m.

■ **3** Turn left (ESE) up a lane. Bend right beneath power-lines. Proceed for 200m.

■ **4** Turn sharp left at a footpath sign amidst rhododendrons. The uphill woodland path passes through a field-gate onto open grassland. Cross a stile adjacent to a field-gate. Go through a field-gate.

■ **5** Turn left up a lane. Bear right through the yard of Home Farm and onto the A595. Cross the road.

■ **6** Turn right (E), passing the entrance to Muncaster Castle on the right. Proceed uphill for 400m.

■ **7** Go straight ahead where the road bends sharply right. Follow a bridleway to Eskdale and Hardknott up the walled Fell Lane (NE). Pass through a field-gate. Continue ahead uphill.

■ **8** Go through a wicket-gate between three field-gates. Pass Muncaster Tarn on the left. Continue uphill. Go through a gate at the top of the rise.

■ **9** Fork left off the path up a bankside at a plantation corner on the left. A narrow loop path meanders up to the OS triangulation pillar and cairn on the summit of Hooker Crag (231m/758ft).

SECTION B	2.8 miles (4.5km)	
Destination	Irton Road Station (GR 139999)	
Ascent	40m(131ft)	Descent 211m(692ft)

■ **10** Go ahead from the cairn for 20m. Turn sharp right (SE). Follow a downhill path. Cross a depression to join the main path.

■ **11** Turn left (ENE), bending right round a broad marshy area on the left. The boggy path rises gradually between rocky outcrops. Continue to a huge flat stone table at Ross's Camp.

■ **12** Go ahead on a downhill path, down to a marshy depression. Bend right through a gap at a wall corner. Continue ahead along a wall on the left. Bend right, away from the wall, skirting marshy ground. Go up an incline. Descend the path ahead.

■ **13** Pass through a kissing-gate on a narrow plateau. Continue ahead (E) to a pathway junction.

■ **14** Turn left (N), passing through a field-gate on approaching a white house. The path becomes a walled lane. Pass over a railway bridge to the junction at Irton Road Station on the right.

SECTION C	4.2 miles (6.7km)	
Destination	Burnmoor Lodge (GR 183041)	
Ascent	240m(787ft)	Descent 0m(0ft)

■ **15** Continue down the lane. Filter left along the main road for 100m.

■ **16** Turn right over the road. Go along a road (NE) opposite between houses.

■ **17** Pass through a field-gate. Continue along the road over cross-tracks. Go through a gate ahead.

■ **18** Fork left, off the road, crossing diagonally over a car park. Turn left over a footbridge at a bridleway sign to Wasdale Head.

■ **19** Immediately fork right. Follow a rough track uphill (NNE) away from the river. Filter right (NE) at a bridleway junction. Proceed for 0.6 miles. Enter the yard of Low Place Farm through a field-gate. Go between farm buildings.

■ **20** Turn right through a field-gate at the end of the farmyard at a bridleway sign to Wasdale. Follow round a wall on the left for 100m.

■ **21** Turn right over a gated footbridge. Immediately bear left (NE). Pass through two field-gates. Keep ahead with a plantation on the right.

■ **22** Pass through a wicket-gate. Follow ahead at a footpath sign on the right. Ford Black Gill at a wall corner on the left. Go up the bankside, bending right (NE) through two broken walls. Cross a ladder-stile.

■ **23** Turn left, fording the shallow river at the entrance to a ravine. Turn right, upstream (NE), with the river on the right.

■ **24** Turn right, fording the river at the narrowest point. Turn left, following upstream, now with the river on the left.

■ **25** Bear right at a fork near the top of the ravine. Climb away from the river above a combe below on the left. The path becomes indistinct, but bear right (ENE) uphill to avoid boggy ground, making for a clean-cut bracken-line round the base of the hills.

■ **26** Bear left along the bracken-line on the right on a terraced path, contouring, above Burnmoor Tarn on the left. Continue to Burnmoor Lodge.

SECTION D	2.5 miles (4km)	
Destination	Dalegarth Station (GR 174007)	
Ascent	20m(66ft)	Descent 248m(813ft)

■ **27** Turn right from the lodge on a flat path, bending round a hillock on the right. Bear right uphill as far as a junction.

■ **28** Filter right (SSW) onto an old corpse road. The broad cairned path bends right uphill, then descends, bending left to ford Ramshaw Beck. Ahead, pass through a field-gate.

■ **29** Follow (SSW) along a wall on the left. Go through two field-gates. Go ahead through a wicket-gate. Continue downhill (SSW) along a wall to the left. Pass through a wall gap near the bottom. Bear left down a path round an S-bend. Follow the bridleway sign ahead to pass through a field-gate. Go down a short walled lane to a narrow road.

■ **30** Continue on the road. Cross a bridge. Keep ahead on the road through Boot.

■ **31** Turn right at a junction with the main road. Proceed along the main road for 250m.

■ **32** Turn right into Dalegarth Station. Take the Ratty Train on the Ravenglass and Eskdale Railway back to Ravenglass.

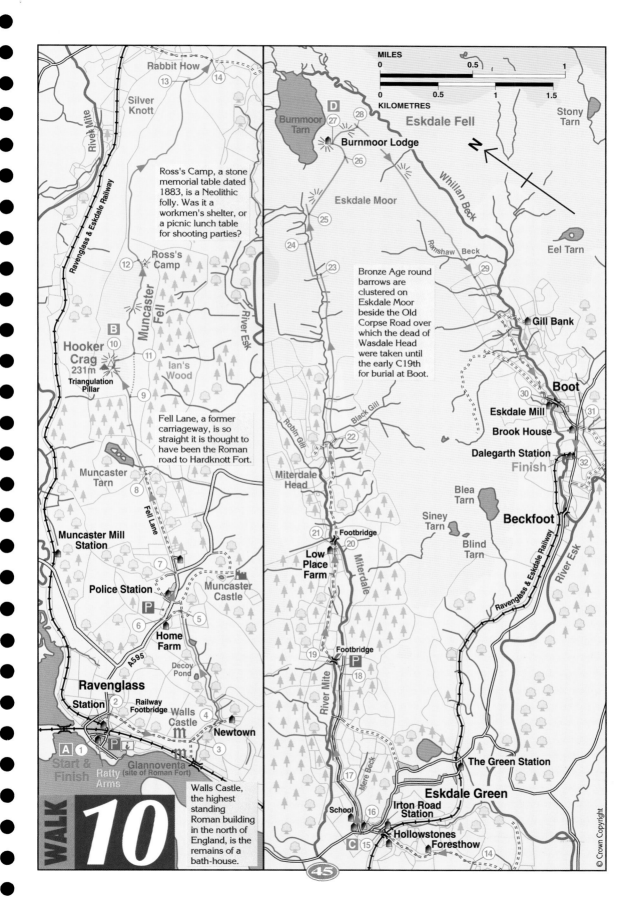

MILES
0   0.5   1

0   0.5   1   1.5
KILOMETRES

Rabbit How

Silver Knott

13   14

River Mite

Ravenglass & Eskdale Railway

Burnmoor Tarn

D   28
27

Burnmoor Lodge

Eskdale Fell

Stony Tarn

N

26

Eskdale Moor

Whillan Beck

Ross's Camp, a stone memorial table dated 1883, is a Neolithic folly. Was it a workmen's shelter, or a picnic lunch table for shooting parties?

Ross's Camp

25

24

Ramshaw Beck

Eel Tarn

12

Muncaster Fell

23

Bronze Age round barrows are clustered on Eskdale Moor beside the Old Corpse Road over which the dead of Wasdale Head were taken until the early C19th for burial at Boot.

29

River Esk

B   10

Hooker Crag
231m
Triangulation Pillar

11

9

Ian's Wood

Robin Gill

Black Gill

22

Gill Bank

30   Boot

31

Eskdale Mill

Brook House

Fell Lane, a former carriageway, is so straight it is thought to have been the Roman road to Hardknott Fort.

Muncaster Tarn

8

Fell Lane

Miterdale Head

21   Footbridge
20

Low Place Farm

Miterdale

Dalegarth Station

Finish

32

Blea Tarn

Siney Tarn

Beckfoot

Blind Tarn

Muncaster Mill Station

7

Police Station

P

6   5

Home Farm

A595

Muncaster Castle

Decoy Pond

19   Footbridge
P
18

River Mite

Ravenglass & Eskdale Railway

River Esk

Ravenglass

Station   2

Railway Footbridge

Walls Castle

4

Newtown

3

A   1

Start & Finish

Ratty Arms

P

Glannoventa
(site of Roman Fort)

Walls Castle, the highest standing Roman building in the north of England, is the remains of a bath-house.

17

Mere Beck

The Green Station

Eskdale Green

School   16

Irton Road Station

C   15

Hollowstones

Foresthow

14

WALK

10

© Crown Copyright

45

11

LOW BIRKER TARN-GREEN CRAG-HARTER FELL-HARDKNOTT FORT-ESK VALLEY

9.7 miles (15.7km)

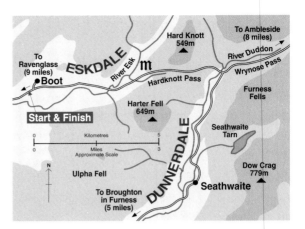

Route Details

Distance	9.7 miles (15.7km)
Degree of Difficulty	Moderate/Strenuous
Ascent	740m (2,427ft)
Time	8 hours

Route Summary

At the heart of this varied walk lies the beauty of the Esk valley, savoured from on high as well as close-at-hand by meandering along the banks of the River Esk. The gradual ascent from the valley floor up an old peat track and over deserted moorland to the summit of Green Crag is delightful. Ahead is the little visited Harter Fell, its three rocky summits distinguishing it as one of the wildest and most distinctive of Lakeland peaks. Lower down, lies the magnificent location of the ruins of the Roman fort of Hardknott Fort, perched on a shoulder, high above the wild country of upper Eskdale with a magnificent panoramic view of the Scafells and stretching down the length of the lower valley as it snakes its way west to Ravenglass and the Irish Sea. Much of the route follows the course of the sylvan River Esk with its deep pools, swirling rapids and rocky gorges. Add to these delights an old packhorse bridge and an isolated church, and a truly fascinating walk is the result.

Start and Finish Points

Dalegarth Station car park (GR 173007). Take the train from Ravenglass on the narrow-gauge railway to the end of the line at Dalegarth Station.

If travelling from the north, turn left (E), off the A595, at Gosforth through Santon, Santon Bridge and Eskdale Green. If approaching from the south, turn right, off the A595, just before Holmrook. Go through Eskdale Green. Keep ahead on the Hardknott Pass road to Dalegarth Station car park on the left.

Coming from the east, follow the long, narrow and very steep twisting road over Wrynose Pass and Hardknott Pass (A good weather route only).

Maps Needed

OS Outdoor Leisure No 6 (1:25 000)
OS Landranger No 89 (1:50 000)
OS Landranger No 96 (1:50 000)

Parking Facilities

Trough House Bridge car park (GR 172002).

Short Cuts

At (8) continue past Low Birker Guest House. Turn left over Doctor Bridge to (26).

At (16) leave Harter Fell (W). Pass (15). Go downhill (WNW). Emerge at either (22) or (24).

At (19) continue down the road, by-passing Hardknott Fort on the right. Proceed as far as (21).

The Roman fort of Hardknott perched above the Esk valley

The walk should only be attempted when the weather is fine and after a dry spell. At such times, it makes route-finding over high ground easier and less prone to marshy conditions.

Interesting Features

GEOLOGY The walk along the River Esk serves as a clear indication of the geological structure of the locality. The grey andesite boulders of the river-bed in the higher reaches are indicative of the Borrowdale Volcanic Series structure of Harter Fell, Crinkle Crags, Bow Fell, and the Scafell range which are situated at the head of the Esk Valley. Progressing downstream, the waters flow over the smooth pink coarse-grained granite where igneous intrusion takes over from the Borrowdale Volcanics.

LANDFORMS Green Crag, between the Duddon valley and Eskdale, is the highest of a serrated string of modest peaks. They rise out of desolate moorland which forms the vast expanse of fell as it stretches seawards (SW) to Black Combe on the outer fringes of Lakeland. Across marshy moorland (ENE) rises the pyramid of Harter Fell, crowned by grey rocky ramparts. Lying between the River Duddon (E) and the River Esk (W), Harter Fell serves as a feeder to both rivers. Its eastern slopes, rising from the Duddon valley, are extensively covered in forest up to a height of 457m (1500ft). Harter Fell occupies a prominent position on a ridge which leads for many miles (SW) towards the sea and to Hard Knott (NE).

HISTORY The Roman name for Hardknott Fort was Mediobogdum. It occupied a strategic position on the road leading east from the port of Ravenglass (Glannaventa) to the twin forts at Ambleside (Galava) and onwards over High Street to Brougham (Brocavum) near Penrith. Built of turf and timber about 117AD and later reconstructed in stone, it is a small fort, which would house less than 500 men. It was abandoned early in the late C2nd when no local threat was apparent and the Romans had given up ideas of a conquest of Ireland from Ravenglass. All that remains is a skeletal reconstruction of the walls. It follows the standard Roman plan with a tower at the four corners of a square walled enclosure and a gateway in the centre of each wall. Outside to the south is the bath-house and furnace, while north-east is the parade ground.

St Catherine's Church probably dates back to the early C12th, though it was extensively restored in 1881. Amongst the interesting tombstones in the graveyard is one to the memory of Tommy Dobson, a once-famous huntsman.

For the history of the Esk valley and the Ravenglass and Eskdale Railway, consult Walk 10 on page 43 (History).

VIEWPOINTS The summit of Green Crag is a splendid vantage-point for views over little Eel Tarn and Burnmoor Tarn (NNW), Stony Tarn to Yewbarrow, Red Pike and Pillar, beyond which in the far distance lies Grasmoor. A rival prospect lies (SW), over the bulk of Black Combe to the Irish Sea, with Devoke Water on a shelf (WSW). Scafell and Scafell Pike lie (NNE) with Esk Pike, Bow Fell and Crinkle Crags (NE). The foreground (ENE) is dominated by Harter Fell, whilst (E) over Seathwaite Tarn are views of the Coniston fells.

Clouds gather over Harter Fell viewed across the Esk valley

There are similar prospects from Harter Fell. By moving to each of its three summit tors it is possible to open up a wide expanse of Lakeland fells. (N) the Scafell range and Upper Eskdale are very prominent, a view which has a closer vantage-point from the Hardknott Fort. There is a superb aerial view (N) of the Roman fort below. Distant views not seen from Green Crag are those (NE) of St Sunday Crag and Fairfield, whilst beyond on the horizon to the right is the High Street range. The Mardale Harter Fell can be discerned (ENE). The eye travels down to the sea via the Esk valley (W) and the Duddon valley (S).

Cross-Section of the Route

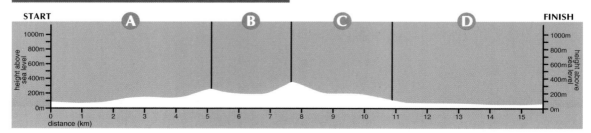

Route Description

(653m/2142ft).

SECTION A	3 miles (5km)		
Destination	Green Crag (GR 200983)		
Ascent	437m(1433ft)	Descent	0m(0ft)

■ **1** Start from the entrance to the car park. Turn right (WSW) along the road for 250m.

■ **2** Turn left (SSE) onto a lane with Eskdale Outdoor Centre on the right at a sign to Dalegarth Falls.

■ **3** Fork left at the lane end at a sign to Stanley Gill/Birker Moor waterfalls. Go through a field-gate. Bend left up an incline.

■ **4** Fork left through a field-gate at cross-paths with a sign to Boot and Upper Eskdale. Follow a grassland path (NE) through a field-gate. Go ahead through woodland. Cross a footbridge. Go through a field-gate.

■ **5** Bear half-right over grassland. Ford a beck. Proceed half-right to a wall corner. Ignore the bridleway sign to the left.

■ **6** Turn left along the wall on the left. Cross over a stile adjacent to a field-gate. Continue ahead with the river below on the left.

■ **7** Pass through a field-gate. Continue (NE), passing a small plantation and tarn on the right. Go through a field-gate at the bottom of the slope. Cross a footbridge. Continue ahead. Ascend a walled path.

■ **8** Fork right (ESE), off the main path where it drops down to Low Birker. Go up a path, bending left to a wall corner. Go through a kissing-gate.

■ **9** Bear right, zig-zagging uphill on a disused peat track. Go ahead at the top, past a ruined peat hut. The track bends left. Bear left, downhill, at cross-paths. Skirt round a marshy plateau to the right.

■ **10** The path leads (SSE) above Low Birker Tarn on the right. Gradually ascend a faint path (SSE) marked by small cairns. Bend left (SE) and (E). Arrive at a boundary stone on a col between The Pike up on the left and Green Crag up on the right.

■ **11** Turn right, then left up the lower slopes of Green Crag. Bend right to the cairn on the summit of Green Crag (489m/1604ft).

SECTION B	1.7 miles (2.7km)		
Destination	Harter Fell (GR 219997)		
Ascent	303m(994ft)	Descent	139m(456ft)

■ **12** Return to the boundary stone at (11). Turn right (ENE). Follow a thin path down a marshy slope. Keep to the left. The path peters out, but go ahead (ENE). Aim for a plantation below Harter Fell.

■ **13** Turn left (NW) along the forest boundary fence.

■ **14** Turn right over a stile waymarked to Harter Fell. Follow up the fence on the right (NE). Bear right at the end of the fence. Ascend a cairned path to a junction with a broad path.

■ **15** Turn right (ESE), uphill, bending left to the triangulation pillar on the summit of Harter Fell

SECTION C	1.7 miles (2.7km)		
Destination	Hardknott Roman Fort (GR 218015)		
Ascent	0m(0ft)	Descent	429m(1407ft)

■ **16** Descend (E) from the summit. Filter left at the bottom of the initial slope onto a broad descending grassy path (NE).

■ **17** Cross a stile in a fence with a plantation on the right. Continue along the fence on the right (NNE). Pass over a stile in a fence and continue ahead.

■ **18** Bear left (NNW) on a level path near the end of the plantation. Filter left onto the Hardknott Pass road. Go downhill for 200m.

■ **19** Bear right, off the road, where it bends sharply left at a low level footpath sign. Proceed (WNW) on a thin path, aiming for the north corner on the square wall surrounding the fort. Turn left, along the north-western boundary wall. Turn left, along the south-western wall.

SECTION D	3.3 miles (5.3km)		
Destination	Dalegarth Station (GR 172007)		
Ascent	0m(0ft)	Descent	172m(564ft)

■ **20** Turn right at the south corner of the wall. Descend the fell (SW) to a wall corner on the right. Filter right down the road to a cattle-grid.

■ **21** Turn left at a bridleway sign. Cross Jubilee Bridge. Bend right through a kissing-gate. After 25m, go through another kissing-gate ahead.

■ **22** Immediately fork right (WSW), downhill, along the wall on the right. Leave the wall briefly. Go uphill through a kissing-gate. Continue ahead.

■ **23** Ford Dodknott Gill. Cross a stile into a plantation. After 100m, pass over a stile into scattered trees. Ford a gill. Pass through a gate. Cross a footbridge.

■ **24** Turn left with a gill on the left. Bend right away from the gill. Follow a bridleway sign on the right to Penny Hill. Cross a stile adjacent to a field-gate. Go along a wall on the right. Cross another stile adjacent to a field-gate. Go through a field. Pass through a field-gate. Ford a stream. Pass through a field-gate ahead. After 100m, pass through another field-gate. Go along a farm track into the yard of Penny Hill Farm.

■ **25** Pass the farm on the right. Continue ahead (W) on the farm track. Pass through a field-gate. Go ahead over Doctor Bridge.

■ **26** Turn left (SW) at a sign to St Catherine's Church. Cross a stile adjacent to a field-gate. Follow the river on the left. Go through a wicket-gate. After 250m, take the centre of three pathways. Pass through two field-gates, then a kissing-gate.

■ **27** Keep ahead at a junction with the river on the left. Bend left through a kissing-gate. Follow round right.

■ **28** Turn right (N) away from the river. Pass St Catherine's Church on the left. Follow the walled lane to emerge on the road.

■ **29** Turn left along the road for 250m. Turn right into the car park.

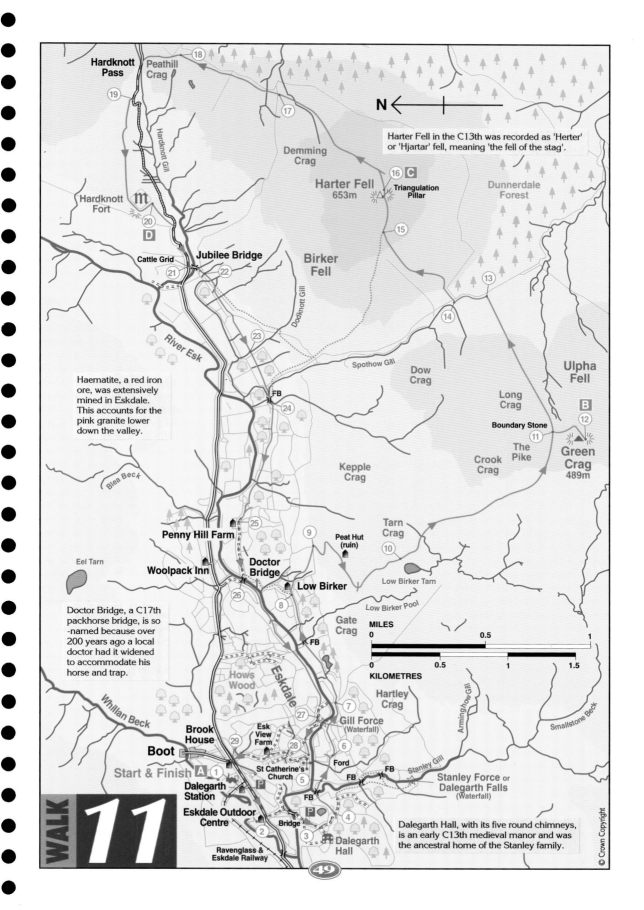

Hardknott Pass

Peathill Crag

18

19

Hardknott Gill

Harter Fell in the C13th was recorded as 'Herter' or 'Hjartar' fell, meaning 'the fell of the stag'.

17

Demming Crag

Harter Fell 653m

16 C

Triangulation Pillar

Dunnerdale Forest

N

Hardknott Fort

20

D

15

Cattle Grid

Jubilee Bridge

21

22

Birker Fell

13

Dodknott Gill

14

River Esk

23

Spothow Gill

Dow Crag

Ulpha Fell

Haematite, a red iron ore, was extensively mined in Eskdale. This accounts for the pink granite lower down the valley.

FB

24

Long Crag

Boundary Stone

B

12

11

Green Crag 489m

Blea Beck

Kepple Crag

Crook Crag

The Pike

Eel Tarn

Penny Hill Farm

25

9

Peat Hut (ruin)

Tarn Crag

10

Woolpack Inn

Doctor Bridge

Low Birker

Low Birker Tarn

Doctor Bridge, a C17th packhorse bridge, is so-named because over 200 years ago a local doctor had it widened to accommodate his horse and trap.

26

8

Low Birker Pool

Gate Crag

MILES
0   0.5   1

FB

KILOMETRES
0   0.5   1   1.5

Whillan Beck

Hows Wood

Eskdale

Hartley Crag

Arminghow Gill

Smallstone Beck

Brook House

27

7

Gill Force (Waterfall)

Boot

Esk View Farm

29

28

6

Start & Finish

A

1

St Catherine's Church

5

Ford

FB

FB

Stanley Gill

Stanley Force or Dalegarth Falls (Waterfall)

Dalegarth Station

P

Eskdale Outdoor Centre

2

Bridge

3

FB

P

4

Dalegarth Hall

Ravenglass & Eskdale Railway

Dalegarth Hall, with its five round chimneys, is an early C13th medieval manor and was the ancestral home of the Stanley family.

WALK 11

49

© Crown Copyright

WALK 12

THE OLD MAN OF CONISTON- DOW CRAG- BUCK PIKE- BROWN PIKE
6 miles (9.7km)

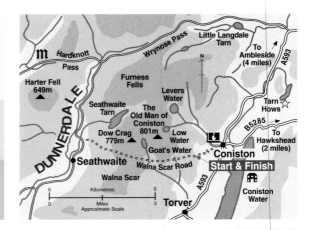

Route Details

Distance	6 miles (9.7km)
Degree of Difficulty	Easy/Moderate
Ascent	652m (2,138ft)
Time	5 hours

Start and Finish Points

Informal parking areas (GR 289971).

140m (S) after the bridge in Coniston village, turn right, off the A593. Go up a minor road signposted to Old Man/Walna Scar/Seathwaite. After 200m, bear left at a fork.

At crossroads, go ahead up a narrow lane at a signpost to Old Man/Walna Scar/Seathwaite and stating 'Unsuitable for motors after half a mile ahead'.

Immediately pass the entrance to the old Railway Station car park on the left. Go to the end of the lane. Pass through a field-gate to park left and right of the Walna Scar Road.

Maps Needed

OS Outdoor Leisure No 6 (1:25 000)
OS Landranger No 96 (1:50 000)

Parking Facilities

There are car parks in Coniston village. The old Railway Station car park (GR 300976) is the nearest to the starting point.

Short Cuts

At (11), turn left at Goat's Hawse. Go down a rocky path along the eastern shore of Goat's Water, gradually descending to (20). Turn left along the Walna Scar Road to (1).

Route Summary

The route avoids the popular tourist path through the debris of abandoned mine-workings. It follows a more remote zig-zag course up the south-east flank of The Old Man of Coniston, via grassy terraces dotted with scented thyme and minute Alpine plants. This gradual ascent affords constant backward views over distant Coniston Water. From the summit cairn of The Old Man of Coniston there is an extensive all-round panorama. A switchback path around a horseshoe ridge leads over the craggy perch of Dow Crag, one of Lakeland's most dramatic peaks, and renowned for the part it has played in the development of rock-climbing. The continuing ridge route along a dramatic escarpment edge provides ever-changing vistas over lakes and tarns to distant mountains, as well as an overview of the broad sweep of the western coastal plain and across the Irish Sea to the Isle of Man.

Walna Scar Road, a former packhorse route, leading into Coniston

The return along the ancient packhorse track of the Walna Scar Road, fringed to the north by remnants of a once-thriving Bronze Age Settlement, supplies a leisurely and scenic finale to an exhilarating walk.

Interesting Features

GEOLOGY The Borrowdale Volcanic structure of the Coniston fells has created lofty ridges, craggy fissures in steep rock walls, scree slopes and boulder fields, waterfalls and tarns. Extensive igneous intrusions meant copper mining and quarrying, which has left a scarred landscape.

LANDFORMS The Duddon and Brathay valleys almost separate the Coniston fells from the other Lakeland mountains, the only narrow link being Wrynose Pass (N).

The Old Man of Coniston is at the southern end of a ridge in a cluster of mountains around the hub of Swirl How. Its downfall (NNE) drops into the dark waters of Low Water, whilst its grassy flank (W) makes a more gradual descent to Goat's Hawse.

Dow Crag, situated almost opposite the Old Man on the horseshoe ridge, is nearly identical in structure. Its vertical wall (E) plunges into Goat's Water beneath, whereas its slope (W) descends gently to the valley of Tarn Beck.

HISTORY Coniston Water, long ago called Thurston Mere, is frequently in view during the walk. It is 5.3 miles long and 56 metres (184ft) at its deepest point. Long and straight, it has seen frequent attempts at the world water-speed record. On 4th January 1967, Donald Campbell disappeared beneath its waters when his Bluebird K7 crashed at 328mph. It was the highest speed ever achieved on water, but could not be made official as the boat never completed the required distance.

The large white house, Brantwood, on the eastern shore of Coniston Water, was the home of John Ruskin, Victorian art critic and philosopher. He bought a derelict cottage in 1871, and transformed it into a glorious house, now open to the public.

Peel Island, near the southern end of the lake, is known as 'Wild Cat Island' in J Arthur Ransome's 'The Swallows and the Amazons'.

Between 1860 and 1940 a steamboat, 'Gondola', operated on Coniston Water. Restored by the National Trust, it now offers a scheduled service.

The slopes (E) of The Old Man of Coniston contain the ugly scar of Coppermines Valley. Copper was probably mined by the Romans, and became very productive in the C16th in the hands of German engineers, employed by the Company of Mines Royal at Keswick. Some mines reached

depths of over 305 metres (1,000ft), but closed at the end of the First World War when the cost of pumping water from the shafts became uneconomical. Some of the slate quarries are still being worked.

View of the Coniston fells from the Walna Scar Road

VIEWPOINTS From the summit of The Old Man of Coniston, the Scafells hold pride of place (NW). On the horizon (S) is a vast seascape, punctuated from left to right by the Kent, Leven and Duddon estuaries. Coastal prominences such as Sellafield Nuclear Fuels Plant, Morecambe Battery, and Blackpool Tower can be discerned. (SW) is the Isle of Man. A multiplicity of tarns are on view: Low Water, Levers Water, Stickle Tarn (NNE); Tarn Hows and two sections of Windermere (ENE); Esthwaite Water and Coniston Water (E); Torver Reservoir and Beacon Tarn (S); and Blind Tarn (SW).

(S) of Goat's Hawse is Goat's Water below, with jagged cliffs rising (W) to the prominence of Dow Crag.

From Dow Crag (NW) are views across the Duddon and Esk valleys, (W) over Devoke Water to the Isle of Man, and (E) to the summit of The Old Man of Coniston.

200 metres along the escarpment south of Dow Crag are awesome views down the plunging gullies to Goat's Water in the valley far below.

Cross-Section of the Route

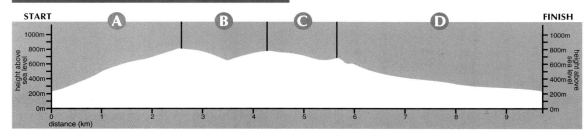

START   A   B   C   D   FINISH

height above sea level

1000m — 800m — 600m — 400m — 200m — 0m

distance (km)   0   1   2   3   4   5   6   7   8   9

Route Description

SECTION A	1.7 miles (2.7km)		
Destination	Old Man of Coniston (GR 273978)		
Ascent	523m(1715ft)	Descent	0m(0ft)

■ **1** Start at a footpath sign to Walna Scar/Dow Crag at the entrance gate to the parking-areas. Go ahead (SW) along Walna Scar Road, a broad stony track which gradually bends right. Proceed to a junction with a mine track, coming down the fellside on the right. Ignore this mine track and continue for 10m.

■ **2** Turn right, leaving the Walna Scar Road, with the tiny reeded Boo Tarn situated opposite, on the left. Go up a clear grassy path alongside a beck on the right with the mine track passed earlier on the far side. Proceed, gradually uphill, for 150m to arrive at a cairn.

■ **3** Bear half-left at the cairn when the mine track opposite bends right. Follow the path away from the beck. Ascend (NW) the broad grassy path with spoil heaps ahead on the right. Proceed to a fork on the path.

■ **4** Do not take the obvious right fork towards the spoil heaps. Skirt round to the left of them, following the cairned path which twists (NW), steadily climbing up the fell, and fording several narrow downcoming rivulets on the way.

■ **5** Bend right on a grassy plateau. Ascend (NE) a shallow gully, going between rocky outcrops. Keep ahead at the top following a faint path along a narrow grassy terrace.

■ **6** Double back left (NW) at the end of the terrace where obscured quarry buildings can be viewed over the hillock to the right. The zig-zagging cairned path continues uphill. Proceed, bending right to emerge at a junction of paths on a grassy saddle on the south ridge of The Old Man of Coniston with Low Water Tarn far below ahead (N) and Brim Fell beyond.

■ **7** Turn right at this junction joining the popular and well defined tourist path from Coniston via a valley of abandoned copper mines. Climb quite steeply (W) on a clear rocky path, bending left, then right. After 400m of ascent, arrive at an OS triangulation pillar and the solid slate platform topped by a cairn on the summit of The Old Man of Coniston (803m/2,634ft).

SECTION B	1.1 miles (1.8km)		
Destination	Dow Crag(GR 263978)		
Ascent	129m(423ft)	Descent	154m(504ft)

■ **8** Turn right (NW) from the cairn, leaving the summit along the eastern edge of the ridge, with Low Water and its surrounding mine-workings now below on the right. Continue along the path for 300m to a fork of paths.

■ **9** Fork left, leaving the main path. Follow a downhill path contouring over the broad open fell, bending left. Proceed for 500m to reach another fork of paths.

■ **10** Filter left (WNW) onto a broad cairned stony downhill path which bends left (WSW) onto the col of Goat's Hawse.

■ **11** Go ahead over cross-paths with Goat's Water seen below on the left. Ascend (W) onto the Seathwaite Fells on a clear rocky path.

■ **12** Bend left (SSW) with sheer jagged rocks dropping down to the left. A relatively easy scramble leads to the narrow cairnless summit of Dow Crag (778m/2,552ft).

SECTION C	1 mile (1.6km)		
Destination	Brown Pike (GR 261966)		
Ascent	0m(0ft)	Descent	96m(315ft)

■ **13** Continue along the path ahead (S) to scramble down from the summit. Bear slightly right through a broken wall after 200m. Keep ahead (S), gradually descending along the edge of the escarpment.

■ **14** Pass Great Gully and Easy Gully on the left. These gullies drop down to Goat's Water far below. Continue up a slight slope to the summit of Buck Pike (744m/2,440ft).

■ **15** Keep ahead on the clear path along the escarpment edge, gradually bending left, then right above Blind Tarn Screes with little Blind Tarn in sight, far below on the left. Ascend a very short slope to the summit cairn of Brown Pike (682m/2,237ft).

SECTION D	2.2 miles (3.6km)		
Destination	Walna Scar Road (GR 289971)		
Ascent	0m(0ft)	Descent	402m(1319ft)

■ **16** Turn right, leaving the the summit cairn. Descend half-left (WSW), down the fell, to reach a pathway junction on the col of Walna Scar Pass (580m/1,902ft) which is Lakeland's fifth highest pass.

■ **17** Turn left onto the Walna Scar Road, following the descending broad track (ESE) for 500m to a left uphill fork.

■ **18** Ignore the left turn and continue ahead, keeping on the track, with Goatfoot Crags up on the left. Continue ahead, winding gradually downhill (E) to Cove Bridge.

■ **19** Cross Cove Bridge over Torver Beck which flows from Goat's Water to feed Coniston Water. Keep ahead, still on Walna Scar Road, bending right, then left, before straightening out (E). It cuts through Little Arrow Moor with Bronze Age settlements well over to the right. Continue along the track to reach a junction of paths coming in from the left.

■ **20** Ignore this path junction and proceed ahead (E), keeping to the track. Continue to reach a fork with a bridleway.

■ **21** Bear left at the fork and continue (NE) along the Walna Scar Road, passing tiny Boo Tarn on the right and proceeding to (2). Retrace the outward route back to the car park.

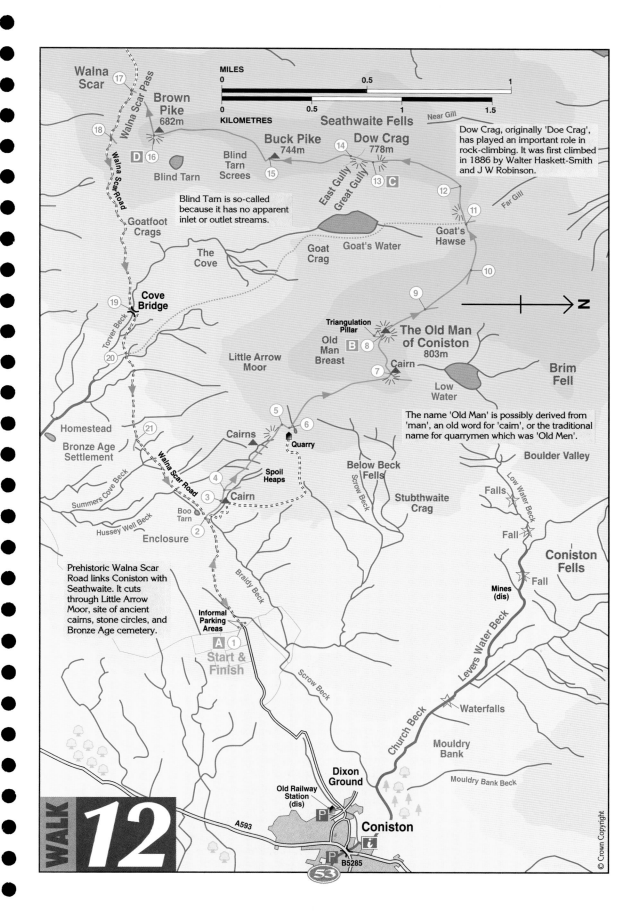

Walna Scar ⑰

Brown Pike
682m

Walna Scar Pass

⑱

Walna Scar Road

Goatfoot Crags

D ⑯

Blind Tarn

The Cove

Cove Bridge

⑲

Torver Beck

⑳

Homestead

Bronze Age Settlement

Summers Cove Beck

Hussey Well Beck

Enclosure

②

③ Cairn

④

Cairns ▲

⑤

⑥

Quarry

Spoil Heaps

Boo Tarn

Walna Scar Road

㉑

Little Arrow Moor

MILES

0   0.5   1

KILOMETRES

0   0.5   1   1.5

Seathwaite Fells

Buck Pike
744m

Blind Tarn Screes

⑮

⑭

East Gully
Great Gully

Dow Crag
778m

⑬ C

⑫

⑪

Goat's Hawse

⑩

Far Gill

Near Gill

Goat Crag

Goat's Water

Dow Crag, originally 'Doe Crag', has played an important role in rock-climbing. It was first climbed in 1886 by Walter Haskett-Smith and J W Robinson.

Blind Tarn is so-called because it has no apparent inlet or outlet streams.

Triangulation Pillar

Old Man Breast

B ⑧

⑨

The Old Man of Coniston
803m

Cairn ▲

⑦

Low Water

Brim Fell

The name 'Old Man' is possibly derived from 'man', an old word for 'cairn', or the traditional name for quarrymen which was 'Old Men'.

Below Beck Fells

Scrow Beck

Stubthwaite Crag

Boulder Valley

Falls

Low Water Beck

Fall

Coniston Fells

Fall

Mines (dis)

→ N

Prehistoric Walna Scar Road links Coniston with Seathwaite. It cuts through Little Arrow Moor, site of ancient cairns, stone circles, and Bronze Age cemetery.

Braidy Beck

Informal Parking Areas

A ①

Start & Finish

Scrow Beck

Levers Water Beck

Church Beck

Waterfalls

Mouldry Bank

Mouldry Bank Beck

Dixon Ground

Old Railway Station (dis) P

WALK 12

A593

P

Coniston

ℹ

P

B5285

53

© Crown Copyright

WALK

13

WETHERLAM-SWIRL HOW-GREAT CARRS-HELL GILL PIKE-BIRK FELL

7.7 miles (12.5km)

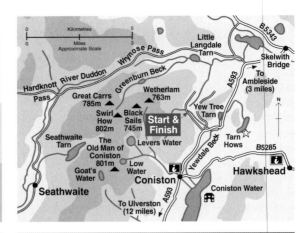

Route Details

Distance	7.7 miles (12.5km)
Degree of Difficulty	Strenuous
Ascent	971m (3,184ft)
Time	8 hours

Start and Finish Points

Car park (GR 306010), near Low Tilberthwaite.

From Ambleside, take the A593 (S), towards Coniston. Fork left over Skelwith Bridge. 0.8 miles after passing Yew Tree Tarn on the right and after a sharp bend in the road, double back right on a minor 'no-through' road to Tilberthwaite.

From Coniston take the A593 (N), towards Skelwith Bridge and Ambleside. After 2 miles fork left, off the A593, onto the minor 'no-through' road to Tilberthwaite.

Follow this road for 0.8 miles as far as the Low Tilberthwaite car park which is met on the left, before crossing Yewdale Beck.

Maps Needed

OS Outdoor Leisure No 6 (1:25 000)
OS Landranger No 90 (1:50 000)

Parking Facilities

The car park is near Low Tilberthwaite. It has no facilities. Nearest services are in Coniston or Skelwith Bridge.

Short Cuts

There are no easy escape routes to any advantage. However, in deteriorating weather retrace the outward route.

Route Summary

This is a spectacular walk, affording aerial views of a multiplicity of peaks and valleys, lakes and tarns. Added interest is provided by a plethora of disused quarries, caves, tunnels and copper-mine shafts on Lakeland's most industrialised mountain, Wainwright referring to them as 'Wetherlam's Hundred Holes'. These abandoned mine-workings, often screened by trees, enhance rather than detract from the scenic beauty of the landscape surrounding the Tilberthwaite valley and fells. A splendid climb up the valley and over the Wetherlam crags, leaves a short steep climb onto Swirl How. Rugged outcrops gradually give way to broad grassy ridges, and a return to the lovely countryside of Tilberthwaite over the shoulder of Birk Fell.

Cottages at Low Tilberthwaite on the lower slopes of Birk Fell

The paths are good, but the walk should be approached with caution: mine-shafts, some of them unfenced, are dangerous and should not be explored; the high rocky ridges are situated on the western edge of the fells where obscuring cloud readily collects. Consequently, the walk should only be undertaken in settled weather if its splendours are to be savoured in safety.

Interesting Features

LANDFORMS Though only 1 metre lower than The Old Man of Coniston, Swirl How is at the geographical centre of the Coniston fells with ridges radiating out to all four points of the compass. The route along its eastern ridge over Wetherlam summit intersects the Greenburn and Little Langdale valleys (N) and the Tilberthwaite and Coppermines valleys (S). From this ridge are views (SW) of the long southern ridge, linking The Old Man of Coniston and Swirl How. The northern scythe-shaped ridge is also in full view rising out of the abyss of the Greenburn valley. The western ridge stretches over Grey Friar into the Duddon valley

HISTORY For the origins and development of copper-mining in the area, consult Walk 12 on page 51 (History).

130 metres south of the summit of Great Carrs, left of the path, is the undercarriage of a Halifax bomber. All seven of its Canadian crew died when it crashed in October, 1944. Flying from west to east it failed to clear the ridge, the undercarriage was ripped off, and the rest of the plane hurtled into the Greenburn valley, where the remains can be discerned, scattered amidst the rocks of Broad Slack below the escarpment edge on the right.

Below the ridge from Wet Side Edge to Rough Crags (N) can be seen the road over Wrynose Pass. It follows the course of the Roman Road which linked the western coastal fort of Glannoventa (Ravenglass), via the fort of Hardknott Pass, with the fort at Galava (Ambleside). From there, the highest Roman road in Britain, continues its easterly course over the High Street ridge to the fort at Brocavum (Brougham) near Penrith.

On Passing through the settlement of Low Tilberthwaite, note the detached National Trust cottage with its spinning-gallery.

VIEWPOINTS Wetherlam, situated away from the main bulk of the Coniston fells, provides one of the best unobstructed Lakeland viewpoints. (NW), across the Greenburn valley, lies Red Tarn in the col between Pike of Blisco and Cold Pike, backed by Crinkle Crags and Bow Fell, with Scafell Pike and Sca Fell beyond to the left; (N) up Little Langdale, over Blea Tarn, is Stickle Tarn and the Langdale Pikes, and in the far distance Skiddaw and Blencathra; (NE) over the course of the River Brathay, takes in Little

Langdale Tarn, Elter Water, and beyond from left to right the Helvellyn, Fairfield, High Street and Kentmere Fells. (E) in the distance is Blelham Tarn with the head of Windermere beyond; (ESE) Tarn Hows and Wise Een Tarn; and (SE) Esthwaite Water fronts the middle reaches of Windermere, beyond which is the long line of the Pennines. (S) the eye travels over Coniston Water, Beacon Tarn and Torver Reservoir, before reaching the Kent Estuary and Morecambe Bay. (SW) is a long escarpment ridge, dominated at its southern extremity by The Old Man of Coniston with Low Water Tarn below, and moving (W) across Brim Fell are the summits of Swirl How, Great Carrs, Little Carrs and Hell Gill Pike at the head of the Greenburn valley.

Coniston Water backed by Coniston village and Wetherlam summit

(W) from Swirl How, over the long flat top of Grey Friar, the British Nuclear Fuels Plant at Sellafield can be seen, and beyond, in clear weather, the Isle of Man. (SSW) is the peak of Dow Crag with Seathwaite Tarn below on the right.

The summit of Great Carrs encapsulates many of the features previously identified, including an enhanced prospect (NW) of the Scafell Range. (NE) the eye surveys the Greenburn valley with its tarn and beck leading to Little Langdale Tarn. The long raking western slopes lead down into the Duddon valley, and (WSW) is a glimpse of Devoke Water.

Cross-Section of the Route

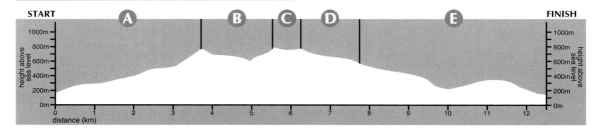

Route Description

SECTION A

SECTION A	2.5 miles (4km)	
Destination	Wetherlam (GR 288011)	
Ascent	612m(2007ft)	Descent 0m(0ft)

■ **1** Start by leaving the south corner of the car park. Ascend steps (W) up the lower slopes of Horse Crag. At the top, turn sharp right on an uphill grassy track. Bend left with disused quarries on the left and Yewdale Beck in the gorge below on the right.

■ **2** Fork left on an uphill path, off the downhill track to the gorge. After 200m, ford a downcoming beck. Scramble up the opposite side. Continue on a path which bends right (SW) round the rim of Tilberthwaite Gorge below on the right.

■ **3** Turn right at the head of the gorge to ford Crook Beck. Go ahead (NNW) on a sketchy path over marshy ground for 200m.

■ **4** Turn right at a deep mine shaft on the left. Cross a footbridge over Tilberthwaite Gill. Immediately double back right up a short incline.

■ **5** Turn sharp left (N) at the top onto a disused mine track. Gradually ascend the valley, bending left to Dry Cove Bottom. The track swings right, passing shallow marshy ground on the left. Bend left to the end of the track at disused mine buildings.

■ **6** Turn right (W) at a small cairn. Climb up to a large cairn at a gap in a wall. Go through the gap onto Birk Fell.

■ **7** Continue up a steep zig-zag cairned path up onto the col of Birk Fell Hawse, with Greenburn reservoir and beck below on the right.

■ **8** Bear left at the junction along Wetherlam Edge to the foot of a steep slope. Many cairns are confusing, but basically keep straight ahead (SW) over boulders and scree to the summit of Wetherlam (762m/2,500ft).

SECTION B

SECTION B	1.1 miles (1.8km)	
Destination	Swirl How (GR 273006)	
Ascent	186m(610ft)	Descent 146m(479ft)

■ **9** Follow a stony path (W) to descend a slope. Bear slightly right, then left across Red Dell Head Moss. Continue following the path (WSW) across Keld Gill Head with the Greenburn valley below on the right, skirting round the slopes of Black Sails on the left.

■ **10** Cross the grassy plateau of Swirl Hawse. Ascend the steep rocky slope of Prison Band (WSW) to the summit of Swirl How (802m/2,630ft).

SECTION C

SECTION C	0.4 miles (0.7km)	
Destination	Great Carrs (GR 271009)	
Ascent	23m(75ft)	Descent 40m(131ft)

■ **11** Go ahead (W), now bending (NW) around the rim of the Broad Slack escarpment on the right. Pass a memorial to an aeroplane crash on the left. Continue ahead (N) to reach the summit of Great Carrs (785m/2,575ft).

SECTION D

SECTION D	1.7 miles (2.8km)	
Destination	Rough Crags (GR 288026)	
Ascent	0m(0ft)	Descent 358m(1174ft)

■ **12** Bear slightly right on a path which soon bends left (NNW) down a rocky slope over a boulder field. After 350m, pass to the left of Little Carrs.

▣ **13** The downhill path (NNW) flattens out, bending right (NNE) round the summit of Hell Gill Pike on the right. Continue ahead along Wet Side Edge.

■ **14** At a cairn, fork right (NE) on a path down a long gently sloping grassy ridge (ENE), gradually bending right (E). Continue along the ridge to the end of Rough Crags (427m/1,400ft).

SECTION E

SECTION E	0.5 miles (0.8km)	
Destination	Greenburn Mines (GR 291022)	
Ascent	0m(0ft)	Descent 200m(656ft)

■ **15** Fork right, off the ridge, opposite the Greenburn mine-workings below on the right. An indistinct path with very small cairns threads a zig-zag course down the fellside.

■ **16** Bear round right (S) as the path levels out. Aim for the mine-workings and Greenburn Beck across gradually descending grassland with no distinct path.

■ **17** Ford the Greenburn Beck above the falls to the right of the extensive disused mine-workings. Bear left to pass through the workings. Emerge at the eastern end onto a broad stony track. Pass a spoil-heap on the left of the track with a large boulder just above on the right and continue for 50m.

SECTION F

SECTION F	1.5 miles (2.4km)	
Destination	Low Tilberthwaite (GR 306010)	
Ascent	150m(492ft)	Descent 227m(744ft)

■ **18** Fork right (E), off the track. Follow a sketchy level path parallel with the track below on the left. It bends right round a grassy hummock, then left at a small rocky outcrop on the right. Gradually ascend the fell (ESE) through bracken. The path sometimes fades, but move gradually right. Ignore any branch paths to the left. Ford Birk Fell Gill.

■ **19** Turn right (SE) along a wall on the left. Climb steeply uphill for 250m, ignoring two ladder-stiles on the left. Pass over a stile in a wire fence. Continue ahead along the wall on the left.

■ **20** After the level crest of the rise, the path descends steeply (SSE) with the wall on the left and a gorge on the right. After descending for 300m, pass over a short section of wooden fencing in a wall gap. Descend over grassland.

■ **21** Go through a field-gate as the path bends round left onto a mine track. Bear right to go through a field-gate. Pass between farm buildings, bending left onto the road.

■ **22** Turn right (SE) along the road. Cross the road bridge over Yewdale Beck to enter the car park on the right.

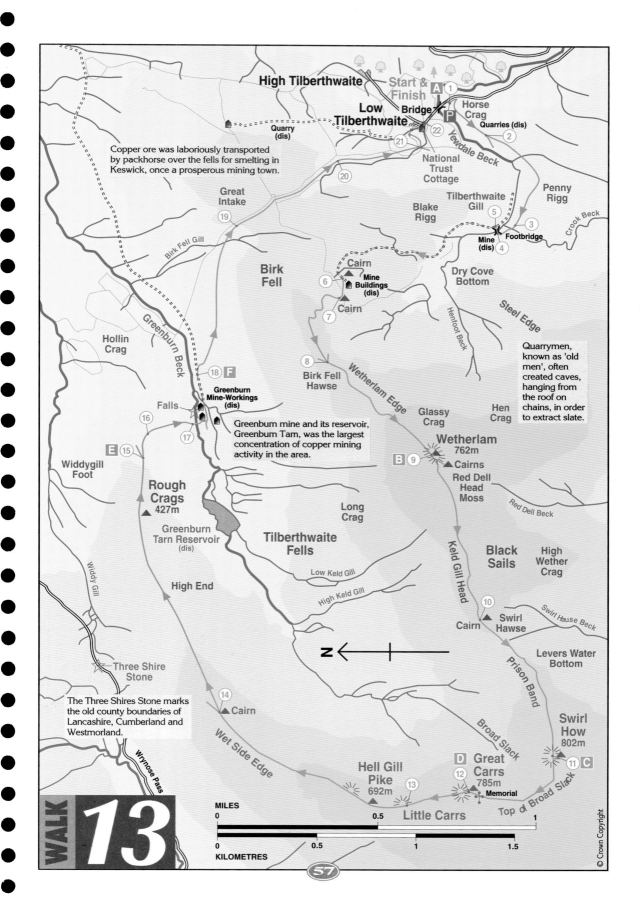

High Tilberthwaite

Start & Finish **A** **1**

Low Tilberthwaite

Bridge

Horse Crag

Quarries (dis) **2**

Quarry (dis)

Copper ore was laboriously transported by packhorse over the fells for smelting in Keswick, once a prosperous mining town.

National Trust Cottage

Penny Rigg

21

22

20

Great Intake

Blake Rigg

Tilberthwaite Gill

5

3

Crook Beck

19

Birk Fell Gill

Mine (dis) **4**

Footbridge

Birk Fell

Cairn

6 Mine Buildings (dis)

Dry Cove Bottom

Steel Edge

7 Cairn

Hollin Crag

Greenburn Beck

Henfoot Beck

Quarrymen, known as 'old men', often created caves, hanging from the roof on chains, in order to extract slate.

18 **F**

Falls

8

Birk Fell Hawse

Wetherlam Edge

Glassy Crag

Hen Crag

Greenburn Mine-Workings (dis)

16

17

Greenburn mine and its reservoir, Greenburn Tarn, was the largest concentration of copper mining activity in the area.

Wetherlam 762m

B **9**

Cairns

Red Dell Head Moss

Red Dell Beck

E **15**

Widdygill Foot

Rough Crags 427m

Long Crag

Black Sails

High Wether Crag

Greenburn Tarn Reservoir (dis)

Widdy Gill

High End

Tilberthwaite Fells

Low Keld Gill

High Keld Gill

Keld Gill Head

10 Cairn

Swirl Hawse

Swirl Hause Beck

Levers Water Bottom

Three Shire Stone

N ←

Prison Band

Broad Slack

Swirl How 802m

11 **C**

The Three Shires Stone marks the old county boundaries of Lancashire, Cumberland and Westmorland.

14 Cairn

Wet Side Edge

Hell Gill Pike 692m

13

D Great Carrs 785m

12 Memorial

Top of Broad Slack

Wrynose Pass

Little Carrs

WALK 13

MILES
0   0.5   1

KILOMETRES
0   0.5   1   1.5

57

© Crown Copyright

WALK 14

YOKE-ILL BELL-FROSWICK-THORNTHWAITE CRAG-MARDALE ILL BELL-HARTER FELL-KENTMERE PIKE

12 miles (19.4km)

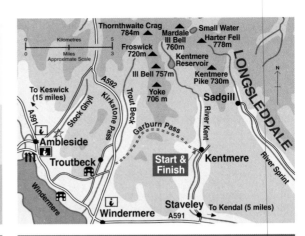

Route Details

Distance	12 miles (19.4km)
Degree of Difficulty	Strenuous
Ascent	1,135m (3,723ft)
Time	9.5 hours

Start and Finish Points

Parking lay-bys in Kentmere (GR 456041).
Midway between Kendal and Windermere, turn off the A591 (N) into Staveley. Bear left out of the village to follow a minor road to Kentmere village.

Maps Needed

OS Outdoor Leisure No 7 (1:25 000)
OS Landranger No 90 (1:50 000)

Parking Facilities

There is limited roadside parking between St Cuthbert's Church and the Village Hall. Nearest services in Staveley.

Short Cuts

At (6) fork left on a loop path which detours round the summit of Yoke. This path can be followed further to bypass the summits of Ill Bell and Froswick, to rejoin the designated route path.

At (10) fork right on a loop path to bypass Thornthwaite Crag and rejoin the main path at (13).

At (15) turn right at Nan Bield Pass. Descend the valley to fork right at Overend. Proceed to (25) along Low Lane. Turn right and follow the route to the parking lay-bys.

At (19) take the first fork on the right, descending the fellside, via Hallow Bank and Brockstones, and rejoin the path at (23).

Route Summary

The Kentmere 'round' is a splendid horseshoe ridge walk across seven summits with dramatic aerial views over wild mountain scenery into lakes and reservoirs, as well as a fine prospect of distant mountains and the coastal plain. Leaving Kentmere, the route follows the Garburn Road, a former packhorse track, onto the ridge at Garburn Pass. Boggy bits are left behind over open moor on an airy, switchback ridge ahead. The summits of Yoke, Ill Bell and Froswick lie on a path before attaining the imposing beacon of Thornthwaite Crag. So far, Kentmere reservoir has occupied attention, to the east. Now, it is the turn of Hayeswater and Blea Water to catch the eye from the northern downfall of another spectacular undulating ridge.

Looking west over C14th Kentmere Hall up to the Garburn Pass

Once over Mardale Ill Bell and across Nan Bield Pass with views of Small Water below, a short ascent of the western slope of Harter Fell, a haunt of wild fell ponies, reveals breathtaking views over Haweswater north of the summit. A return down a broad moorland ridge over Kentmere Pike, with a wall and fence as a guide, once again encounters quiet winding lanes into the hamlet of Kentmere.

Interesting Features

LANDFORMS The Kentmere 'round' traces a horseshoe ridge which encloses a valley containing Kentmere Reservoir and the upper reaches of the River Kent. The western ridge rises from Garburn Pass on a northerly course over the conical summits of Yoke, Ill Bell and Froswick to the top of Thornthwaite Crag and onwards to High Street. The ridge divides the Troutbeck valley (W) from the Kentmere valley (E), the eastern downfall being particularly craggy and steep and characteristic of the Borrowdale Volcanic mountain structure. Thornthwaite Crag serves as a meeting-point of four valleys and the source of four streams: (N) Hayeswater is fed by Hayeswater Gill, whilst (NNW) Pasture Beck flows down Pasture Bottoms, both streams leading into Ullswater; (S) Trout Beck follows a course into Windermere; (SE) the River Kent eventually finds an outlet into Morecambe Bay.

On the ridge east from Thornthwaite Crag lies Mardale Ill Bell whose southern slopes also supply water to the River Kent, though its northern downfall is more spectacular where Blea Water Crag makes a precipitous descent down to pearl-shaped Blea Water. Onward, down over the Nan Bield Pass, the ridge continues up onto Harter Fell which again has a dramatic northern downfall to Haweswater Reservoir in Mardale below.

From Harter Fell, over the rounded Kentmere Pike, the broad western ridge of the 'round' leads (S), serving as a barrier between the Kentmere valley (W) and Longsleddale and the River Sprint (E).

HISTORY There is no pub in Kentmere. The Low Bridge Inn, now a private house, was the first pub in England to lose its licence in the C19th as a result of drunkeness and immorality.

The rutted stony Garburn Road is a former packhorse track over the Garburn Pass, joining the villages of Troutbeck and Kentmere. Its route follows along a thin band of Coniston limestone.

The route briefly touches on the course of Britain's highest Roman road. It stretches over the High Street ridge for about 10 miles at a height upwards of 610 metres (2,000ft). It links the forts of Brocavum (Brougham) near Penrith in the east and Galava (Ambleside). From there it continues west, via the fort on Hardknott Pass, to the coastal fort of Glannoventa (Ravenglass). The ancient Britons probably created the route before the Romans, and in the C13th it was known as 'Brettestrete' (the Briton's road).

VIEWPOINTS All high-level horseshoe ridges passing over several summits have the advantage of providing a continuous viewpoint, each summit revealing more or less the same views of distant mountains. Therefore, a general direction-finder must suffice. (N) is the High Street range; (E) over the Shap Fells are the Pennines fronted by the Howgill Fells to the right. (SE) it is possible to discern distant Ingleborough. (S) the Kent Estuary and Morecambe Bay is in the background fronted by a section of Windermere (SSW); (SW) the Old Man of Coniston and Swirl How occupy the skyline with Wetherlam in front of them. (W) is the serrated edge of Crinkle Crags and the pyramid of Bow Fell with the Scafell range and Great Gable behind them; (WNW) lies Dove Crag and Fairfield; and (NW) is the Helvellyn range behind St Sunday Crag with Blencathra to the right away in the distance.

The church at Kentmere, a hamlet with neither shop nor pub

Descending from Thornthwaite Crag there is a fine aerial view of Hayeswater below on the left. Likewise from the Mardale Ill Bell and Harter Fell summits there are worthwhile short strolls (N) for bird's-eye views down into Blea Water and Haweswater.

Cross-Section of the Route

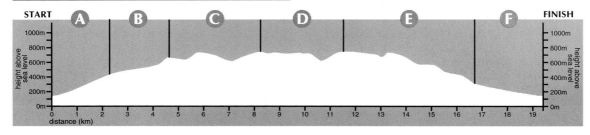

Route Description

SECTION A	1.5 miles (2.4km)		
Destination	Garburn Pass (GR 437044)		
Ascent	287m(941ft)	Descent	0m(0ft)

■ **1** Start by continuing up the road (N), bending left over a bridge. Proceed to the road end at a farm.

■ **2** Turn right at a public bridleway sign to Troutbeck/Garburn Pass. Follow up a stony farm track, bending left (W). Pass through a field-gate. Continue ahead (W) on the terraced track.

■ **3** Pass through a field-gate. Ahead, go through a gateway. Cross a footbridge. Pass through a gap between wall corners. Climb open fell, bending right (WNW), then left (SW) to join a wall on the left. Go through a field-gate at the top onto Garburn Pass (447m/1,466ft).

SECTION B	1.5 miles (2.4km)		
Destination	Yoke (GR 438067)		
Ascent	259m(850ft)	Descent	0m(0ft)

■ **4** Turn right along a wall on the right. The path gradually climbs the ridge (N) for 1 mile (1.6km) keeping fairly close to the wall.

■ **5** Cross a ladder-stile at a wall corner. Bear right and bend left (N) on a stony uphill path.

■ **6** Fork right up to the south summit cairn of Yoke (706m/2,316ft).

SECTION C	2.4 miles (3.8km)		
Destination	Thornthwaite Crag (GR 432101)		
Ascent	321m(1053ft)	Descent	233m(764ft)

■ **7** Continue ahead to the north cairn. Descend to cross a depression. Go along the escarpment edge on the right. Ascend the slope (N) to the summit of Ill Bell (757m/2,483ft).

■ **8** Continue on a zig-zag path which bends left (NW) steeply down the escarpment edge. Cross a depression at Over Cove, bending right (N). Ascend the slope to the summit of Froswick (720m/2,362ft).

■ **9** Leave the summit at an iron fence-post on the left. Descend on a zig-zag path (NW), bending right (N) over a col. Climb the slope along intermittent iron fence-posts on the left.

■ **10** Fork left (NNW) up onto Thornthwaite Crag (784m/2,572ft).

SECTION D	2 miles (3.3km)		
Destination	Harter Fell (GR 460093)		
Ascent	199m(653ft)	Descent	195m(640ft)

■ **11** From the beacon follow a broad downhill path (ESE), bending left round a depression.

■ **12** Fork right (NE) off the main path onto a thin path. Go towards a wall corner ahead, the path bending right of it.

■ **13** At a junction, continue ahead, swinging right below the summit of Mardale Ill Bell (760m/2,493ft).

■ **14** Filter right onto a path, descending steeply, bending right, then left to Nan Bield Pass.

■ **15** Go ahead (ESE) over cross-paths to climb steeply a rocky zig-zag path. Pass over a series of shelves ascending to the summit of Harter Fell (778m/2,552ft).

SECTION E	3 miles (4.9km)		
Destination	Longsleddale Bridleway (GR 476049)		
Ascent	69m(226ft)	Descent	517m(1696ft)

■ **16** Turn right (SSW) at the cairn on a path along a wire fence on the left. Pass over The Knowe. Descend (S) over Brown Howe and skirt round a boggy depression. Ascend to the summit of Kentmere Pike (730m/2,394ft), marked by an OS triangulation pillar over the wall.

■ **17** Stay (SE) on the path along the wall, later a wire fence, for 800m.

■ **18** Take the middle of three forks at a cairn, leaving the fence on the left. Continue ahead (SSE) over open fell for 400m.

■ **19** Pass over a high ladder-stile. Continue ahead (S) along a wall on the left, ascending to the summit of Shipman Knotts (587m/1,925ft).

■ **20** Continue downhill (S) along the wall. Pass through a broken wall. The narrow path descends steeply between the wall and short rock buttresses. Skirt right around a marshy plateau, bending left to rejoin the wall on the left. Pass through a broken wall onto Wray Crag.

■ **21** Bend left, zig-zagging downhill (SE) with the wall on the left. The path swings right (S) away from the wall near the bottom. Cross a shallow beck onto the Longsleddale cart-track bridleway.

SECTION F	1.6 miles (2.6km)		
Destination	Kentmere village (GR 456041)		
Ascent	0m(0ft)	Descent	190m(623ft)

■ **22** Turn right on the winding bridleway track (W) down the valley. Pass through a field-gate after 1 mile. The track bends left downhill, then right to pass a barn on the right. Proceed along a walled track (W), bending right (N). Pass through a field-gate. Go ahead downhill, bending left (NW).

■ **23** Turn left (SSW) along the High Lane. Pass through a field-gate. Proceed for another 100m.

■ **24** Turn right over a stile at a footpath sign. Continue (WSW) on a downhill field path. Go over a stile.

■ **25** Cross Low Lane to pass over a stile opposite. Follow the field path (WSW) downhill. Cross a footbridge. Pass through a kissing-gate. Ahead, pass through a stepped wall gap.

■ **26** Turn left (SSW) on a walled lane. Pass through a field-gate with two barns on the right. Go through an enclosure with a farmhouse on the right. Go through a field-gate.

■ **27** Fork left on the main track. Pass through a field-gate. Continue down a driveway, passing the church on the right.

■ **28** Turn right (W), uphill, on the road to the parking lay-bys.

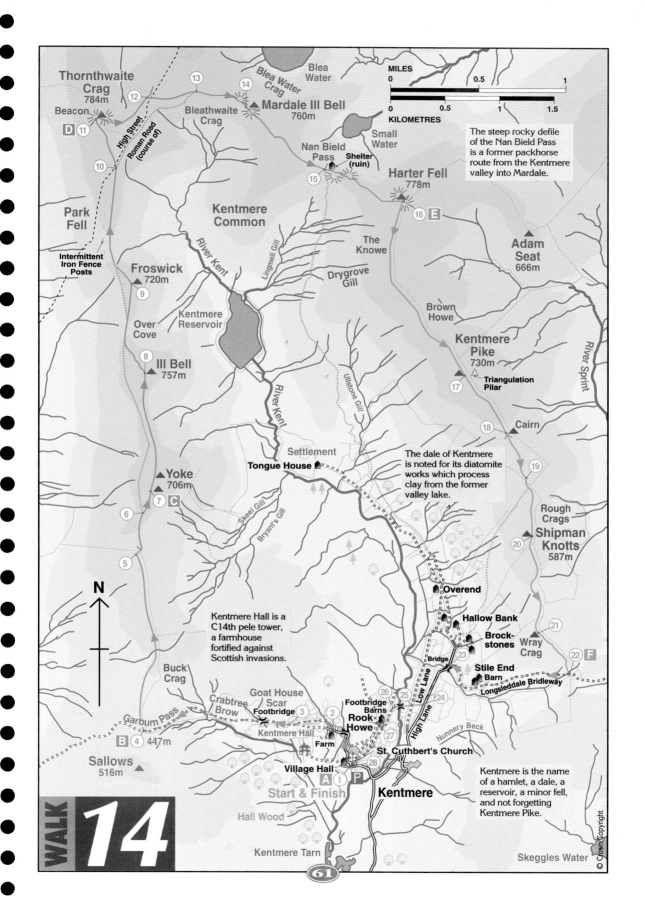

MILES
0   0.5   1

0   0.5   1   1.5
KILOMETRES

Thornthwaite Crag 784m
⑫
Beacon
D ⑪
High Street Roman Road (course of)
⑩
Park Fell
Intermittent Iron Fence Posts
Froswick 720m
⑨
Over Cove
⑧ Ill Bell 757m

⑬
Bleathwaite Crag
Blea Water Crag
Blea Water
⑭ Mardale Ill Bell 760m

Nan Bield Pass
Shelter (ruin)
⑮

Small Water

Harter Fell 778m
⑯ E

The steep rocky defile of the Nan Bield Pass is a former packhorse route from the Kentmere valley into Mardale.

Kentmere Common

River Kent
Lingmell Gill

The Knowe
Drygrove Gill

Adam Seat 666m

Brown Howe

Kentmere Pike 730m
⑰ △ Triangulation Pilar

River Sprint

Kentmere Reservoir

River Kent

Ulstone Gill

⑱ Cairn

The dale of Kentmere is noted for its diatomite works which process clay from the former valley lake.

⑲

Yoke 706m
⑦ C
⑥
⑤

Settlement
Tongue House 🏠

Rough Crags
Shipman Knotts 587m
⑳

Skeel Gill
Bryant's Gill

Overend 🏠
Hallow Bank 🏠
Brock-stones
Bridge
㉓
Stile End Barn
Longsleddale Bridleway

㉑
Wray Crag
㉒ F

Buck Crag

Crabtree Brow
Garbum Pass
B ④ 447m

Goat House Scar Footbridge
Kentmere Hall
Farm

Footbridge Barns
③ ② Rook Howe
Low Lane
㉖ ㉕ ㉔
㉗
High Lane

Nunnery Beck

Kentmere Hall is a C14th pele tower, a farmhouse fortified against Scottish invasions.

St. Cuthbert's Church

Sallows 516m

Village Hall
A ① P
㉘

Kentmere

Kentmere is the name of a hamlet, a dale, a reservoir, a minor fell, and not forgetting Kentmere Pike.

Start & Finish

N

Hall Wood

Kentmere Tarn

Skeggles Water

© Crown Copyright

WALK 14

61

WALK 15

FAR SAWREY-MOSS ECCLES TARN-WISE EEN TARN-THE HEALD-CLAIFE HEIGHTS

7.4 miles (12km)

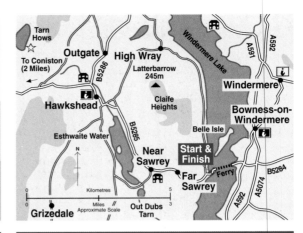

Route Details

Distance	7.4 miles (12km)
Degree of Difficulty	Easy
Ascent	438m (1,436ft)
Time	6 hours

Start and Finish Points

Car park (GR 388954) in Station Scar Wood.
From Bowness-on-Windermere take the ferry across Windermere. From the terminal proceed (S) on the B5285 for 500 metres and the car park is on the right.
From Hawkshead follow the B5285 (S) and the car park is on the left 500m before the ferry terminal.

Maps Needed

OS Outdoor Leisure No 7 (1:25 000)
OS Landranger No 96 (1:50 000)

Parking Facilities

Car park (GR 388954) at the starting point.

Short Cuts

At (15) turn right. Follow a winding path (SE) through forest to (21). Bear right to follow the designated route.
At (18), instead of turning right, continue ahead (E) descending a winding setted track and passing Belle Grange on the left. Turn right (S) on a track along the western shore of Windermere. The track becomes a narrow tarmac road. Arrive at (25) and continue to the car park. This is a short cut in terms of time rather than distance, substituting lakeside views for high level views over Windermere.

Route Summary

This fine scenic walk passes through countryside beloved of Beatrix Potter and a source of inspiration in her writings. Claife Heights is quite thickly wooded with a blend of native woodland and conifer plantations. However, there is extensive open fell dotted with rocky tors and small tarns, contrasting with fertile farmland on its lower slopes. Especially attractive are the breathtaking aerial views over Windermere from the wooded terraced path along the eastern escarpment edge of the fell. The varied topography ensures a rich mixture of plants and trees which thrive on acidic soils, and in their turn they provide a habitat for a wide variety of bird and animal life. A quiet approach can afford a glimpse of red deer browsing or drinking from tarns which are nesting-sites for coots and mallards, which in their turn attract the predatory fox, stoat and mink.

Windermere from the Bowness ferry terminal at Far Sawrey

The circuit is undemanding in terms of ascent and the paths are good throughout. It requires sufficient time to explore its intriguing landscape features, observe its native wildlife, and take in the views of Windermere and distant mountains.

Interesting Features

GEOLOGY The northern Lake District is dominated by Skiddaw Slates, ancient sedimentary rocks thrust up to form high rounded tops. Central Lakeland is characterised by the Borrowdale Volcanics, hard solidified lavas resistant to erosion which have produced a craggy landscape. The soft flatter landscapes of southern Lakeland are derived from the Silurian series, shales and grits which were deposited on a sea bed. The thickness of these marine deposits, averaging about 4,573 metres (15,000ft), is amazing considering that over time a top layer has eroded away. Within this vast thickness there are some variations in resistance to erosion, so that small rocky tors protrude from low-lying basins, some containing minor tarns. It is this sort of scenery which characterizes Claife Heights. 'Claife' is derived from 'kleif' (a ridge of cliffs), cliffs which no longer exist as a result of glacier movement smoothing out the contours.

LANDFORMS The rolling hills, tors, tarns and woodland of Claife Heights are bounded to the east by Windermere and to the west by Esthwaite Water. The composition of the soils on the top layer of the Silurian shales has produced a rich variety of acid-loving plants and trees which in their turn serve as a habitat for a wide range of animals and birds.

HISTORY The countryside around Claife Heights inspired the fertile imagination of Beatrix Potter (1866-1943) to create her children's books. From the royalties on her first book, 'The Tale of Peter Rabbit', she purchased C17th Hill Top farm at Near Sawrey where she lived from 1913 until her death in 1943. Further writing success enabled her to buy more Lakeland properties, so that in her will she bequeathed fourteen farms, numerous cottages and 4000 acres of land to the National Trust, who also own Hill Top which is open to the public.

Windermere gained its name from Vinandr or Winland, a Norseman. It is 10.5 miles long and first became an important waterway for the Romans when they occupied the fort of Galava at Ambleside at the head of the lake. Quarried stone, iron ore and charcoal were shipped down the lake for centuries.

Belle Isle is the largest of Windermere's fourteen islands. Formerly known as Long Holm, it was renamed after Isabella Curwen who purchased it in 1791. On it is a unique Georgian round house built in 1774 on the site of a former Roman villa. Wordsworth in 'The Prelude' described it as a 'pepper-pot', as the domed house forms a perfect circle. It has 20 bedrooms, all of which connect as it has no corridors.

For centuries a ferry has plied between Bowness-on-Windermere and The Ferry House on the opposite shore. In October 1635 forty-seven people were drowned on their way home from a wedding and fair. Legend has it that the ferryman was anxious that there should be no more deaths, but one dark stormy night he heard the eerie voice of the 'Crier of Claife' calling to him. Terrified, he never recovered and died shortly afterwards. It was believed that an evil spirit possessed the lake, until a monk exorcised it on a site of what is now a small quarry in the woods to the north, and marked on OS maps as 'Crier of Claife'.

Station Scar Wood on the fringes of Windermere lake

VIEWPOINTS Though Claife Heights attains only about 220 metres (722ft) at its highest point, it is remarkable for the views from its eastern escarpment edge (E) over Windermere as far as the distant hills of the Howgills and the Pennines. (W) can be seen the peaks of The Old Man of Coniston and Wetherlam, and (NW) are the distinctive outlines of the Langdale Pikes. (NE) is Wansfell Pike with Red Screes to the left and High Street, Froswick and Ill Bell to the right.

Cross-Section of the Route

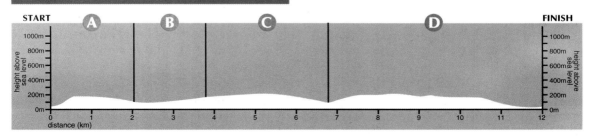

Route Description

SECTION A	1.2 miles (2km)		
Destination	Far Sawrey (GR 379954)		
Ascent	180m(590ft)	Descent	136m(446ft)

■ **1** Start at the north end of the car park at a footpath sign to Claife Heights/Hawkshead. Pass through a forest bar-gate. Proceed along a woodland path for 100m.

■ **2** Turn left at a post with a white waymark. Go up some steps.

■ **3** Turn left at the top of the steps. Bend right to the top of a rise. Pass through a stone archway adjacent to a ruined building. Bear left up a winding woodland path. Follow the white-topped posts.

■ **4** Turn right (NW) at a sign to Hawkshead. The path levels out with views over Windermere to the right. Cross over high grassland with scattered trees. Enter woodland through a broken wall. Pass through a kissing-gate to emerge onto a walled bridleway.

■ **5** Turn left (SW) to follow the footpath sign to Hawkshead/Sawrey. Pass through a gate at the corner of the wood on the left. Bending right, continue ahead for another 100m.

■ **6** Pass through a field-gate at cross-paths. Follow ahead (SW) the sign to Far Sawrey on a bridleway field path, descending and bending left (SSE). Emerge on the B5285 at a telephone kiosk in Far Sawrey.

SECTION B	1.2 miles (2km)		
Destination	Moss Eccles Tarn (GR 373968)		
Ascent	80m(262ft)	Descent	0m(0ft)

■ **7** Turn right along the road. Pass the Sawrey Hotel on the right. Proceed for another 150m.

■ **8** Turn right (NW), off the road, at a bridleway wall sign to Colthouse. Go up a 'no-through' tarmac lane for 350m. Pass through a kissing-gate adjacent to a cattle-grid. Go ahead up a driveway for 100m.

■ **9** Fork left (NW) at a sign to Hawkshead. Cross over a footbridge. The path ascends more steeply, passing over a stile adjacent to a field-gate. Pass over a stile adjacent to a field-gate at a pathway junction at the top of the rise.

■ **10** Go straight ahead (NNW) on the broad bridlepath signposted to Claife Heights. Ignore branch paths. The walled track bends right (NNE) to pass through a field-gate. Ford a shallow rivulet. Proceed to the north-east corner of Moss Eccles Tarn on the left at the top of the rise.

SECTION C	2 miles (3.2km)		
Destination	Above Belle Grange (GR 385988)		
Ascent	68m(223ft)	Descent	116m(380ft)

■ **11** Bear right from the tarn on the uphill path for 50m. Bear left at a fork. Proceed for 200m.

■ **12** Bear left on the path at a waymarked fork, ignoring the field-gate ahead. Pass through a field-gate. Bend right (N) over grassland. Descend over a marshy depression between Wise Een Tarn on the left and an unnamed tarn on the right. The path bends right (NNE) as it climbs.

■ **13** Pass over a stile adjacent to a field-gate at the top of the rise. Enter a conifer plantation. Keep straight ahead on the waymarked track which bends right with the small Highs Moss Tarn over on the right in the trees. Proceed for another 150m.

■ **14** Bear right down the main path (NE) at a pathway junction with a high wire fence on the left.

■ **15** Proceed round a left bend at a path junction on the right. Go downhill for another 130m.

■ **16** Bear right (ENE) on the main path at a junction. Follow a ground-level sign on the right to Belle Grange. Descend, fording Belle Grange Beck. Arrive at signposted cross-paths at the bottom of the path with a high wire fence on the left.

■ **17** Turn right (ENE). Go across a forest track onto a bridlepath. Ford Belle Grange Beck. Descend the forest path, with Belle Grange Beck on the left behind a broken wall, to a path junction on the right.

SECTION D	3 miles (4.8km)		
Destination	Station Scar Wood car park (GR 388954)		
Ascent	110m(361ft)	Descent	186m(610ft)

■ **18** Turn right. Follow a narrow woodland path. Ford a shallow stream. Immediately bear up right at a fork on the stony path. Proceed for 300m.

■ **19** Bear right (S) at a fork. Ascend with a high wire fence on the right onto the ridge ahead. The path levels, passing through bracken with views over the lake to the left.

■ **20** Pass through a gap in a broken wall. Turn right through a gap between two posts of a wire fence inside the wall. Follow the waymarking down through conifer trees, bending left on a broad stony path.

■ **21** Follow a sign to Ferry/Sawrey at a right junction to Hawkeshead. Turn left, 20m ahead. Go through a wall gap at a white-topped waymark post onto a rocky promontory for views over Windermere. Return to the main path. Turn left down a steep winding rocky path. Emerge from the forest with grassland to the right and a high wire fence and wall on the left. Proceed (SSW) on a track for 150m.

■ **22** Pass through a field-gate. Continue uphill. Enter open grassland through a field-gate. Continue (SSW) along a wall on the left. Bend left to descend between walls to (6). Turn left at cross-paths at a sign to Belle Grange. Retrace (NE) part of the outward route, passing (5). Continue for 100m.

■ **23** Pass through a field-gate. Ahead, descend a woodland path towards the lakeshore for 250m.

■ **24** Double back right (SSE) at a pathway junction. Go down a broad descending path through conifers.

■ **25** Turn right on a narrow lakeshore road to pass a castellated gateway on the right. Emerge onto the B5285. Go ahead along the road for 150m.

■ **26** Turn right through an unmarked gap in a low wall. Bear left through trees to the car park.

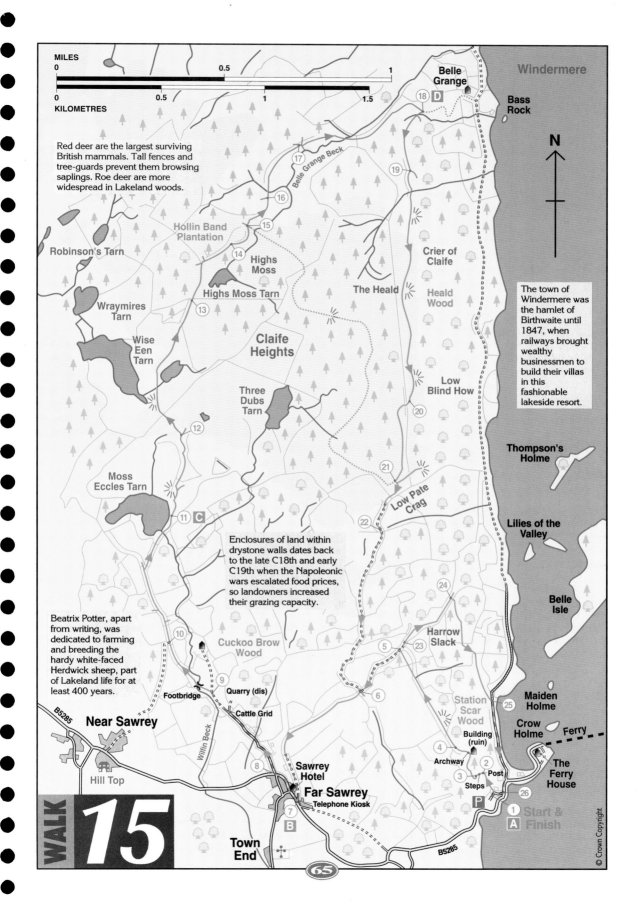

MILES
0   0.5   1

KILOMETRES
0   0.5   1   1.5

Windermere

Belle Grange

Bass Rock

Red deer are the largest surviving British mammals. Tall fences and tree-guards prevent them browsing saplings. Roe deer are more widespread in Lakeland woods.

Belle Grange Beck

Hollin Band Plantation

Robinson's Tarn

Highs Moss

Highs Moss Tarn

Crier of Claife

The Heald

Heald Wood

Wraymires Tarn

Wise Een Tarn

Claife Heights

The town of Windermere was the hamlet of Birthwaite until 1847, when railways brought wealthy businessmen to build their villas in this fashionable lakeside resort.

Three Dubs Tarn

Low Blind How

Thompson's Holme

Moss Eccles Tarn

Low Pate Crag

Lilies of the Valley

Enclosures of land within drystone walls dates back to the late C18th and early C19th when the Napoleonic wars escalated food prices, so landowners increased their grazing capacity.

Belle Isle

Harrow Slack

Beatrix Potter, apart from writing, was dedicated to farming and breeding the hardy white-faced Herdwick sheep, part of Lakeland life for at least 400 years.

Cuckoo Brow Wood

Footbridge

Quarry (dis)

Cattle Grid

Near Sawrey

B5285

Wilfin Beck

Hill Top

Station Scar Wood

Building (ruin)

Archway

Maiden Holme

Crow Holme

Ferry

Sawrey Hotel

Far Sawrey

Telephone Kiosk

Post

Steps

The Ferry House

P

Start & Finish

Town End

B5285

65

WALK 15

© Crown Copyright

Walking & Safety Tips

It is absolutely essential that anyone venturing out into the countryside, particularly hilly terrain, be correctly prepared to reduce the risk of injury or fatality. No amount of advice could cover all possible situations that may arise. Therefore the following walking and safety tips are not intended to be an exhaustive list, but merely a contribution from our personal experiences for your consideration. **We would certainly suggest that inexperienced hill walkers should never consider the routes featured in our publications** and would also advise them to initially participate in a series of guided group walks such as those arranged by various rambler groups.

Clothing & Equipment

The lists represent the basic equipment required to enjoy a full day's hill walking, reasonably safe and comfortably.

CLOTHING:- Strong, sensible footwear - preferably boots with a good sole, strong trainers/lightweight boots can be worn during prolonged dry weather, warm shirt, fibre pile jacket, warm woollen sweater, windproof/waterproof anorak with hood and leggings (several thin layers insulate more adequately than one layer), woollen gloves; woollen hat or balaclava, warm trousers (avoid denim/jeans which become very clammy and cold when wet. This could lead to exposure), and good quality woollen socks or stockings, protected by waterproof gaiters.

EQUIPMENT:- Good compass and maps of the areas, along with a survival bag, whistle or torch for implementing the International Distress Signal - 6 long blasts/flashes in quick succession followed by one minute pause then repeated (the answering signal is 3 blasts or flashes). A basic first-aid kit should also be carried, which contains - bandages, sticking plasters, safety pins, scissors and some gauze pads. Take a rucksack to carry your equipment in, and some food for a butty stop, plus some extra food for emergency rations - chocolate, fruit cake, cheese and dried fruit.

Preparation & Procedure

Ensure that yourself and the others are adequately equipped and that no-one is overburdened. Learn how to use your map and compass competently. You should always be able to at least locate yourself on a map. Find out the weather forecasts for the area. Always consider the wind chill factor - even the gentlest of winds can reduce effective temperatures to a dangerous level. Plan both the route and possible escape routes beforehand

balancing terrain, weather forecast and the hours of daylight against experience whilst allowing for a safety margin. Always try to plan your walk so the prevailing wind is behind you. Always try to walk in company. It is safer and more enjoyable. Gain a basic understanding of first aid. Try to leave written details of your route, point of departure, number in your group, destination and estimated time of arrival. In an emergency this information could save a life. Maintain a steady rhythm, at the pace of the slowest walker. Take care when you are walking to avoid sprains. Be very careful where you step and remain extremely vigilant about avoiding the adder, Britain's native poisonous snake. Take regular breaks - mainly to check your progress and the next stage. Keep an eye on the weather. Always be prepared to turn back if necessary. On completion of your journey inform the person with whom you left your written information of your safe arrival.

Stay Wise - Stay Alive

First aid on the hills requires both knowledge and common sense. If in doubt concentrate on the comfort and morale of the casualty. **IN AN EMERGENCY: STOP AND THINK - DO NOT PANIC.** If you are lost - check your surroundings carefully and try to locate yourself on your map. Find shelter and decide whether it is safe or best to use an escape route. If someone is injured, or is showing the signs of exposure - i.e. stumbling and slurred speech, shivering, irrational behaviour or collapse and unconsciousness, **STOP IMMEDIATELY**, prevent further heat loss, find shelter and place the casualty into a survival bag with extra clothing. Huddle together as a group and give the casualty some warm food and drink. **DO NOT:** rub the casualty, give alcohol, allow further exposure. Decide then on your next course of action. Do you go for help? or do you stay put overnight sending out the International Distress Signal? If you have to stay put overnight try and find or make adequate shelter, conserve food and drink, keep morale high, keep the casualty warm, dry and conscious, and use the International Distress Signal. If you are able to leave someone with the casualty whilst two of your party go for help from a village or farm the following information is essential; accurate location of the casualty, nature of injuries, number injured, number in group, condition of others in group (If one person is suffering it is possible that others will be too), treatment already given, and time of accident. **ALWAYS BE PREPARED FOR THE WORST** and remember that **WET + COLD = EXPOSURE.** If these conditions go unchecked, by not having the correct knowledge and equipment, then they can lead to rapid cooling of the inner body core which will, in turn, lead to exposure, the most common cause of death on the hills. **TO CONCLUDE, YOU MUST BE FULLY PREPARED AND EXPERIENCED.**